GW00870206

Hangings, Sinkings and Trust in God

Life and Death onboard British Warships in the 1700's and 1800's

Text and pictures copyright 2014 Peter Brent

Contents

Introduction

Background: How the Royal Navy came to dominate the World

There Go the Ships, Part One, Chapter 1, 1774 – 1798

Chapter II 1798 – 1837

Part II

Part 2 Chapter I

Part 2 Chapter II

Part 2 Chapter III

Part 2 Chapter IV

Part 2 Chapter V

Part 2 Chapter VI

Introduction

Did you know?

Until 1812 the British Royal Navy would seize Americans and force them into British military service. This was one of the causes of the war between Britain and the US between 1812 and 1815 (see Pressgangs, below).

Did you know?

British seamen in the eighteenth and nineteenth centuries were extremely badly paid, but by helping to seize foreign ships they could earn rewards equivalent to a million dollars or more in modern terms (see Five Hundred Pounds Prize Money, below).

Did you know?

If Napoleon had been one year older he would have been Italian, his parents were Italian, his first language was Italian and he hated the French - at least in his younger life (see Napoleon Bonaparte below).

Did you know?

Canadian Sir Provo Wallace served for 96 years with the Royal Navy (see Sir Provo Wallis below).

"There Go the Ships" was written by the Reverend George E.A Shirley in 1889. It is a fascinating first hand insight into life onboard various British warships between 1793 and 1837.

Actually, the biography is not that of the good reverend, but of his father, who bizarrely is nowhere named in the book. After he retired, Reverend Shirley's father recorded notes about his life at sea. The notes had been misplaced, but fortunately for history were found when the reverend moved house.

"Hangings, Sinkings and Trust in God" draws upon the original text of "There Go the Ships," adds modern historical text to fill in gaps, adds insight and interest to an already fascinating book. Together the two show how random chance can create fascinating, sometimes very diverse connections. The original text is reproduced indented and in a different font, so the reader can easily differentiate it from the new.

Rev. Shirley wrote his book in two parts. The first, other than a few lines at the end, is the complete and unedited notes left by his father. Part two was "compiled from looser memoranda, which it was necessary to add to bring the story to a finish." Whilst part one is wonderful to read, part two seems often pointless, being mainly the thoughts of the reverend, based on content of little interest. "Hangings, Sinkings and Trust in God" therefore draws on the whole of the first part, plus a few selected extracts from the second. For completeness at the end you will find the full text of part two.

Background:
How the Royal Navy came to dominate the World

King Henry the Eighth commenced the process of enlarging and improving his navy, which was to culminate in enabling the carving of the British Empire, the largest empire in history. At its peak it incorporated a third of Planet Earth's landmass. From around its inception in 1707 (when the English and Scottish fleets were combined as a result of the Act of Union) till into the Second World War, The Royal Navy was the largest navy in the world. The massive expansion of the U.S. Navy after Pearl Harbour finally pushed the British navy into second place. It is now ranked fifth after the navies of The United States, Russia, China and Japan.

Until Henry's father, Henry the Seventh set one up, England had no regular navy. Instead, whenever a monarch wished to fight a war or defend England, he had to borrow merchant ships. Henry VIII inherited a navy consisting of five (or seven depending on your source) warships. By the time of his death he had increased this to 40. He did still need to pressgang merchant ships to fight any wars, never-the-less this force formed a professional core on which to base an effective fighting force.

Britain has always enjoyed a certain degree of protection against foreign invasion, thanks to being an island separated from the European mainland. Within continental Europe invasions have proliferated and borders historically constantly shifted, as the only reasonably significant natural barrier to movement of armies has been major rivers. Even at the closest point, invasion of Britain requires a 21 Mile sea crossing.

The English Channel is a good but not complete protection against invasion, as a powerful enemy could still land a substantial army at any place on the coast. Henry was aware of this and feared invasion by the then superpower, Spain. He was also wary of France, understandable as England still occupied part of France (Calais). French dislike of the English was hardly surprising. What he feared most was that these two most powerful countries might combine against England. He realised that England could be reasonably safe even without a large standing army, as long as it possessed a powerful navy. That way any invasion force could be sunk even before it landed its troops. Henry, building on the concept begun by his father, was the real initiator of the force that was to give England (hence later the United Kingdom) nearly complete security from invasion. This led to him being known as the "Father of the English Navy." Although he made a good start, it was to be around two hundred years till the Royal Navy became large enough to offer that near complete protection.

The Royal Navy did not just provide this protection, but was also the lynchpin in allowing Britain to carve out the largest empire in history.

It was in the middle of this long period of Britannia ruling the waves that Mr Shirley Senior penned his account of life in the Royal Navy.

There Go the Ships:
Part One, CHAPTER I, 1774 - 1798

I was born either in Lambeth or Westminster, October 29th, 1774 and lived and worked in both places for some time at a printer's near Lambeth Marsh Turnpike Gate. I remember Astley's Amphitheatre, a large wooden building entered by a wooden bridge over a ditch from the road.

Lambeth or Westminster?
Registration of Births and Deaths

Nowadays, anybody in the UK (and really worldwide) should know where they were born, as since 1837 it has been legally required to record every birth and death. Perhaps Mr Shirley Senior's parents had died young without telling him. Perhaps they just forgot. Either way, it seems likely his birth had not been registered.

The Births and Deaths Registration Act of 1836 set up the framework to implement registration. The mechanism was enabled through the poor-law unions, which existed to provide support to the poor. This "support" was not generally very popular, as it consisted of sending poor people to workhouses: harsh and cruel places similar to prison where incumbents would have to work for the food they received. Fear of ending up in the workhouse was a good (though not complete) deterrent to people claiming in the first place as once families (including their children) were in the workhouse, it was difficult to obtain release back to normal paid employment.

Lambeth Marsh Turnpike Gate

How fascinating to suppose from the description "Marsh" and the feel of the wording ("entered by a wooden bridge over a ditch from the road") that then this place was little more than open country. Now it is the site of Waterloo Station, one of the largest and busiest stations in London. The Marsh still survives in name only. There is a Lower Marsh leading along parallel with the side of the station; also an Upper Marsh. Part of this passes under the railway.

Astley's Amphitheatre

This was a massive permanent covered circus, built in 1773 by Philip Astley. Just one year later, the theatre burnt down. Rebuilt in 1795, the second building was to last until 1803, when it too burnt down. This third and final reincarnation burnt down in 1841. This time it was not rebuilt, and the manager, Andrew Ducrow allegedly died mad as a result, having lost pretty well everything including his faithful old servant in the fire.

> Being of a somewhat restless disposition, I resolved to go to sea, and accordingly entered on board the Courageux, 74, Captain A. Gardner, some time in 1791 as a boy and landsman, and was at sea about eighteen months, when we came home, and I was paid off, and returned to London for a short time.

Courageux

This was a French warship, launched in 1753 and captured in 1761 by the British ship HMS Bellona. The British recovered and repaired her and pressed her into service, retaining her original French name.

She was wrecked off Gibraltar in 1796.

> But the National Assembly of France, on February 3rd, 1793, declared war against the King of England and the Stadtholder of Holland. So to

avoid being taken by pressgangs, I walked to Portsmouth (*over 70 miles / 110km) in company with others to enter the naval service of my country and receive the bounty.

Trafalgar Tavern, Park Row, Greenwich, London

Pressgangs

The Royal Navy had such trouble recruiting sufficient sailors, it used "Impressment," popularly termed "the Press," to capture men and force them into service. Press Gangs were the personnel on land, members of the Impress Service, who carried out this function.

Impressment was used from 1664 (two years before the Great Fire of London) until as late as 1814. Suitable targets were seamen between 18 and 45, especially merchant seamen and including some foreigners. Non-seamen were at some risk, though generally were rarely impressed.

The practice was very unpopular, being considered "un-British," although not stopped by the courts as it was judged vital to the survival of England, then later the UK. Rival navies at the time commonly used conscription, rarely used in Britain. In reality there is little difference morally, except that if you were careful you could legally avoid impressment (basically don't get so drunk you pass out), where to avoid conscription was and is generally illegal.

Wages on Royal Navy ships were very poor, half that of merchant ships and less than those of labourers at the time. Pay was sometimes up to 2 years in arrears, with six months pay kept in hand to discourage desertion. Wages were not increased between 1653 and 1797, until a mutiny forced an increase. Death in service was common. It is no wonder that there were insufficient volunteers.

The system caused considerable tensions between Britain and the United States, as in the opinion of Britain, American born citizens were still British subjects, hence were liable to serve in the British armed forces. This was one of the causes of the war between the two countries between 1812 and 1815.

We were well entertained on the road, the farming men flocking to the roadside inns to hear us sing some sea songs, arriving at Portsmouth February 8th, and joined the St. George, 98 guns, Admiral Gill and Captain Thomas Foley.

The St. George

The St. George was one of eight ships at various times carrying that name in the Royal Navy. Launched in 1785, she was sunk in 1811 off Jutland: later to be the 1916 scene of the largest sea battle of World War One, arguably the largest in history. Almost all of her crew was lost. Fate is clearly the most important factor in life, that if Mr Shirley Senior had not in the meantime transferred to another ship, he probably would have been drowned in 1811.

We sailed from Spithead April 8th, accompanied by three 74-gun ships, and one frigate with sealed orders, to be only opened when we arrived at a certain latitude. On the fourteenth, six days after sailing, the man at the masthead said two sails were in sight; gave chase at 6 a.m., and at 1 p.m. came up with them, and captured both. They proved to be the St. Jago Spanish treasure-ship, having on board seven hundred chests of silver dollars and gold doubloons. She had been taken after a stubborn fight by the General Dumonier, a French privateer, who were so intoxicated with their success, that they did not hurry to get home, and thus lost their prize. We exchanged the crews, making them prisoners, and sent the prizes to Spithead with the Edgar, 74. When they arrived, and the news spread, there was quite a rejoicing among the inhabitants, and the Jews were on the look out to advance money to the crew if they could get the captain's signature, but he refused. The treasure was landed under a strong guard, and sent to London in twenty-one wagons, escorted by a squadron of horse-soldiers, to the Tower of London. We sent the prisoners home in the Ganges and Phoeton, ourselves and the Egmont sailing for a cruise off the Western Isles to join Lord Hood's fleet.

The taking of a Spanish galleon or treasure-ship was quite a notable event in olden times. Strange stories are told of the freaks of sailors to get rid of their money, receiving so much that they did not know what to do with it. They were well said "To earn their money like horses, and spend it like donkeys." One of these treasure-ships that was taken gave an ordinary seaman the modest sum of five hundred pounds prize-money; and of course it was resolved that every man should have two watches, in what were called fob-pockets, one each side of the waistband of the trousers, with a ribbon and a key and bunch of seals; then it was resolved that each should have gold lace on their hats.

Five hundred Pounds prize-money

At this time, a labourer in England earned £12 per annum. Current wage (2013) for a farm labourer is around £16,800 (depending on grade), so in these terms £500 in 1800 money would be equivalent to around £700,000 now (that's about $1 million). For those few lucky enough to gain such a prize and sensible enough to not waste it, such an amount could provide a very healthy retirement as soon as their service was finished (assuming they survived, of course).

It appears the use of the term "modest sum of" was rather tongue in cheek!

One day, one of the crew was seen approaching the ship in a shore-boat with a silver-laced hat. The crew appointed two of their number to wait upon the first lieutenant and ask him to stop such a mean fellow from coming on board, and disgracing the ship's company. But the sailor, seeing the storm that was brewing, and not at all favourable to him, asked to have a word of explanation. This was granted, and standing up in the sternsheets of the boat, he said, "Shipmates, I have tried everywhere to get a gold-laced hat, but could not get it; therefore I made the hatter take the same price for this." They saw that he had not done it to save his money meanly; therefore they asked permission for him to come on board.

After joining Lord Hood's fleet, we rendezvoused at Gibraltar with eighteen sail of the line and frigates to cruise off Toulon, the French having thirty-four sail of the line in the harbour. In August the Spanish fleet joined us, when all the small arms men (of which I was one) were landed to garrison the forts in the name of the French king. The united English and Spanish fleets sailed into the harbour, but might have been stopped, had it not been for an altercation between the first and second in command, one ordering the men to fire on the advancing ships, and the other not to fire. During this time the combined fleet were all in, and resistance was useless, for their broadside would have cleared the batteries from the inside of the harbour.

Lord Hood

Samuel Hood, First Viscount Hood (1724 – 1816) had a long and highly successful career in the Royal Navy, rising from Midshipman to Admiral. During times of peace he was a Peer of the Realm and politician including a period as MP for Westminster.

Whilst a midshipman he served with George Rodney; also later to become a famous admiral. Both had ships named after them which fought in the Second World War. The Rodney, launched in 1925 was becoming rather old when the war started (1939). However, as a heavy 16" gunned battleship, she was to survive the war. The Hood, the pride of and flagship of the Royal Navy, was a little older, launched in 1920. She was a lighter armed (15" guns) and more lightly armoured, but faster battlecruiser. She was famously sunk by the German battleship Bismarck at the Battle of the Denmark Strait. There were 3 survivors from her compliment of 1418.

Admiral Rodney

Samuel Hood served in a number of wars, commencing with the Seven Years War: later as a Captain (HMS's Grafton then Vestal) from 1756. Next he fought in the American War of Independence, followed by action opposing the French Revolution.

Samuel's younger brother was Alexander Hood. He sailed with James Cook (the first captain to circumnavigate and map New Zealand, and first to find the eastern coast of Australia). He served in the same campaigns (but on separate ships) as Samuel. Two of their uncles also served with distinction in the Royal Navy.

During the time I was employed garrisoning the forts, our ship sailed to Genoa, and captured the Modesta Republican frigate, then returned to Toulon. During the first three weeks I was on shore had no change of clothing until the ship returned, then I got a supply. Our admiral was going home in the Minerva; ordered us to sail for Gibraltar. Whilst paying there heard that Toulon was captured by the Republican troops storming it at every point, being very numerous, and Napoleon Buonaparte first signalised himself there as an artillery officer.

Napoleon Bonaparte

As Mr. Shirley Senior writes, Napoleon at this time was merely an artillery officer. Note his changed spelling to the norm (Buonaparte). In fact this is the Italian spelling. Later he spells the name the conventional French way. Very cosmopolitan.

Napoleon was born in 1769 on Corsica, one year after the Island was taken over by the French from the Italians. If that had not happened, he would arguably have been Italian. In fact, some assert (including Napoleon himself when younger) that he was Italian: both his parents were Italian and he was conceived before the French takeover. In his early life he hated the French as the invaders of his homeland.

Napoleon initially spoke only Italian. He started to learn French when he was eight years old. Even by the time he commenced officer training in France, his French remained fairly limited. He retained his heavy Corsican accent throughout his life.

Napoleon of course made the French army the most effective in the world, being beaten eventually only by the (fragmented) opposition of the rest of Europe.

Before the French Revolution, the French Navy also had been massively successful, coming close to challenging the Royal Navy. Who knows whether, but for the revolution it may not have replaced the British navy in the top spot? As it happened, the revolution finished the French Navy as an effective fighting force.

Napoleon tried desperately to bring his navy back to the situation where it could again challenge the Royal Navy. He knew the importance of being able to safely move armies by sea without opposition. However, he was only partially successful, his navy winning a few minor battles and skirmishes. After his death the French navy did continue improving, eventually becoming the great force it had been before the revolution. However, reaching number one was to elude it, the French Navy never supplanting the Royal Navy.

> Toulon was full of Royalists, that is, supporters of Louis, the French king, who had been executed, and they took refuge on board the fleet, that hastened to get out of the harbour, the boats bringing away as many as they could, the Republican soldiers ruthlessly slaughtering the remainder. Lord Hood, before evacuating, burnt the arsenal and fifteen line of battle ships, bringing away eight. The admiral now left us, and going on board the Leviathan, sailed for England.

> After the evacuation of Toulon, an English captain, who knew nothing of the recapture, sailed towards evening inside the harbour, not noticing the tricolour flag, which was hanging drooping, there being not much wind. He quietly dropped anchor, when a French officer came alongside in a boat, ascended to the quarterdeck, and demanded the surrender of the ship, explaining all the news of the recapture of Toulon by the Republican forces. The English captain expressed his surprise at this intelligence, and the French officer replied," Such is the fortune of war." The English captain asked him politely to step into the cabin and partake of some refreshment "over the fortune of war," and to

learn fuller particulars of the capture. He found means to let the first lieutenant know the state of things, and to do his best whilst he engaged the French officer's attention (who was a military man). The cable was quietly slipped, the topsails unfurled, and drifting with the tide out of the harbour, the batteries being only manned with sentinels, as it was nearly dark. No suspicion was aroused until she was outside, when the drums beat to quarters, and the forts opened fire. But the wind freshening, she put such a distance between her and the forts that their fire was harmless. The noise of the drums and artillery fire startled the French officer, and he asked what was the cause, and was told they had run out, and if he wanted to return to Toulon the boat was ready for him. He was indignant at the deception practised upon him, and described it in no measured terms, but received the cool reply, "Such is the fortune of war."

Whilst we were at dinner orders came for us to convey a fleet of transports, with troops on board, up the straits to Leghorn. Sailed in January. When off Cape La Gotti fell in with Commodore Keith Elphinstone, with the Pompeii, Puissant, and others going to Gibraltar. We arrived at the island of Corsica, landed troops in St. Fiorenzo Bay, took St. Fiorenzo with one frigate, and burnt another.

Puissant

The Puissant, not surprisingly from her name, had been a French warship. She was captured by Admiral Lord Hood in 1793. In fact her captain, Mon. Ferrand, had handed her over without a fight, for which the British government awarded him a pension of £200 per annum.

After brief active service she was laid up at Portsmouth as a receiving ship. A receiving ship was one generally too old to withstand service at sea, as its structure would be too weak to weather a storm. The most common use was to house sailors after training but before allocation to a serving ship, likewise with sailors who had been impressed, or as hospital ships. Often ships spent more years in such use than actively at sea.

In the days of sail, when a ship was captured, its crew would share in the value of the seized ship and goods or treasure aboard her. See "prize-money" above. In fact the crew of the Puissant shared prize money three times whilst she was at Portsmouth, even without leaving the port! The custom was that when a ship was captured, any other ships nearby at the time shared the prize, even if they weren't involved in the capture. The lucky Puissant along with other nearby ships gained each time when captures were made in the port itself or close by.

Then we cruised about off Toulon, and at other places on the coast--
sometimes at Leghorn with the fleet, and at other times cruising with a
squadron.

In March 1795, whilst at anchor in Leghorn Roads, we received the
intelligence that the French fleet was out, sailed, and fell in with them
on the 12th, and had a kind of running fight until the 14th, when it
became nearly general, and the two French ships, the La Ira and the
Censuar, were taken. During this time and up to 1796 we chased them
several times into harbour, not being able to bring them to a general
action. In one of the chases the Timoleon, 74, was burnt.

In the beginning of 1796 Sir John Jervis came out from England in the
lively frigate, and took command of the fleet. We proceeded to closely
blockade Toulon, during which time our ship went into Port Ajazzio to
water and repair our rudder, which was done in three days. Whilst
cruising so long the fleet was obliged to go down to St. Fiorenzo to refit,
and surrender the island to the French, not being able to keep it, the
Corsicans having declared for the French Republic. We had been
assisting General Paoli and the patriots previously to secure their
independence. We sent away all the shipping that was in the bay to
Elba.

Sir John Jervis, 1st Earl of St. Vincent

was so obsessed with the idea of serving at sea as a child that he ran
away to join up at the age of thirteen (in fact others joined even
younger). He returned home after a short service but later rejoined,
eventually rising to the rank of First Lord of the Admiralty (i.e. arguably
Commander in Chief of the Royal Navy, the post Winston Churchill later
held from the beginning of World War Two until becoming Prime
Minister).

He was a strict disciplinarian, equally so against his men and his officers,
which was respected. On one occasion he had two men hanged for
mutiny on a Sunday. Another admiral (Thompson) complained to the
Board of the Admiralty, not about the act of hanging, but that the
sentence was carried out on the Sabbath. He stated that Jervis should
be relieved, or if they refused they should relieve him instead. Indeed,
that is what they did; they relieved Thompson.

On another occasion, the crew of the Marlborough refused to hang one
of their number accused of mutiny. Jervis had the rest of the fleet
surround the Marlborough and train their guns on her. He warned he
would sink the Marlborough if the sentence were not carried out. It was.

He could also be kind.

One example of his kindness was once having given his men permission to jump in the sea to swim, one of his ordinary seamen failed to remember that a considerable sum of money was in his back pocket. It consisted of prize money and several years' wages he had been saving, in total £70, perhaps six years' wages at the time. The money was destroyed by the seawater. On realising what had happened, the man started crying. Having enquired what the problem was, in front of the whole ship's crew Sir John refunded the lost money from his own funds.

Another example was when he heard that an orphanage dedicated to the children of sailors who had lost their lives for their country had run out of money. He invited fifty of his officers to dine with him; then asked them to donate funds for the orphanage. Sir John and his officers raised £1000.

As First Lord of the Admiralty, Sir John tried to crack down on corruption within the Royal Dockyards. Publicly because they feared bad publicity, in reality because senior ministers were involved themselves, the Government appointed a powerless board of inquiry. Later Prime Minister Pitt forced Jervis to resign. Jervis was later reinstated, though no longer as First Lord of the Admiralty.

One reform in which he was successful was in greatly improving dockyard efficiency. This was by mechanising the yards with block making machinery designed by Samuel Bentham and Marc Isambard Brunel (the builder of the Thames Tunnel and father of Isambard Kingdom Brunel, famous ship, railway, bridge and tunnel builder).

Sir John retired with a seat in the House of Lords, though he rarely sat there. He became a heavy benefactor to charities, including £500 for survivors of the Battle of Waterloo and £300 for the starving in Ireland. Again displaying his uncharitable disciplinarian side, one issue he was active in within Parliament was that of opposing the abolition of slavery.

> During one of the times we were in the bay the La Ira, one of the captured ships, caught fire by accident, and was burned one evening.
>
> While we were getting the shipping ready for Elba the French and Spanish fleets came in sight; but it appeared that they did not see us, we being under the high land. Afterwards they fell in with a severe gale, were much injured, and compelled to run into port to refit, during which time our fleet got ready, and each with a ship in tow sailed for Gibraltar, all hands being on short allowance, and showing no lights in the night, that we might not be seen, arrived safely at Gibraltar, where we got some provisions.
>
> In November 1796, during which time we had a severe gale for a fortnight, obliged to put on a dry shirt every night, being on the poop from daylight until dark. In the height of the gale the Gibraltar, 80, the Zealous, 74, Courageaux, 74, parted from their cables, and went out of

the bay. The Gibraltar struck upon a rock, and had to go to England in a leaky condition; the Zealous struck on a rock, heeled over, and took it away in her bottom; the Courageaux struck under Apes Hill, and went to pieces, a number of her crew perishing, those who were saved being sent to Lisbon by the Moors.

During the time the Zealous was lying in the Gut, with the rock in her bottom, the Spanish fleet went through in distress, one large ship with her mainmast gone. When the gale ceased we sailed for Cadiz, where we saw the ship without her mainmast safe in the harbour. Then we sailed for Lisbon, eleven sail of the line. Whilst going into Lisbon the Bellerophon, 74, got on the Sands and was lost, but her crew were saved. At Lisbon the Queen of Portugal gave us all a week's allowance of provisions to fill our empty bellies, for we were nearly starved.

Bellerophon

Launched in 1786, broken up in 1836, Bellerophon's claim to fame was that it was onboard her that Napoleon surrendered. Following his defeat at Waterloo, he was attempting to escape to the United States. He was stopped by the blockading Bellerophon.

If the Bellerophon had been a person, she would then have been a rather offended hero, as that was her last action before she was laid up and converted to a prison ship. She was renamed, her new name being apt to her having sent Napoleon into captivity, as it was "Captivity."

She is remembered in a number of folk songs, under her nickname, "Billy Ruffian." Another nickname she had was "The Flying Bellerophon" as she was noted as having an impressive turn of speed.

The name Bellerophon comes from the Greek warrior who rode the winged horse Pegasus. Billy Ruffian was the nearest the common sailors could get to pronouncing her name.

In common with most ships at the time, life onboard was cheap. For instance in the Battle of the Nile she found herself fighting the far bigger French flagship, the Orient. By the end of the battle, Bellerophon had lost 57 dead and 140 wounded. At one stage during the battle all but one of the ships five lieutenants was either dead or incapacitated. On another occasion malaria struck the ship's crew and again 57 died. At the Battle of Trafalgar, she lost 27 dead.

On January 21st the fleet sailed to cruise off Cadiz, being joined by several ships from England. In the evening, just as our ship was crossing the bar, she grounded on the South Sand about 7 p.m., it being reported that it was the pilot's fault. We had all sail set, hove all aback, but it was no use; she being hard and fast amidships. As it was high water she would strike heavy aft and not forward, and at low water lay quite still. All hands went to work, unbent sails, down yards and topmasts, unshipped the rudder by striking hard, made signals of distress, and sent a boat to Lisbon for help, when the next day the St. Albans, 64, came down, and moored on the bar, the wind being off the land. We then hove the launch overboard, spare spars, hencoops, etc., cut away the fore and mizzenmasts, the sails, provisions, guns, carriages, etc., being put into schooners, and sent to Lisbon with much toil and trouble. Whilst on shore the Prince of Portugal came to see us. We were in a miserable plight. On the third night, about eight o'clock, made signal for the St. Albans to heave, we heaving also. After two or three thumps off she went. The next morning the wind changed to off the shore, and had we remained until that time she would soon have broken to pieces.

Went up to Lisbon to get ready to dock. The Zealous, heaving down, had the rock taken out of her bottom, having gotten out her stores, etc. The English fleet arrived, bringing with them the San Joseph, 120, San Salvador, 120, Pytchly, 80, St. Isidore, 74, Admiral Jervis having fallen in with the Spanish fleet of thirty-seven sail of the line and frigates, whilst he had fifteen sail of the line and frigates. By skilful manoeuvring he succeeded in breaking their line, and capturing the four ships named above. Commodore Nelson, in the Captain, 80, succeeded in capturing two, boarding the San Joseph through the quarter gallery or W.C., and seizing the guns run them in. He boarded them crying," Victory or Westminster Abbey," then turned them round, so as to rake the deck fore and aft. They surrendered at once.

Nelson

Nelson was another great admiral (perhaps the UK's finest) who started service young. He first served on a ship at the age of 12 and was a captain already at the age of 20. As much as so many sailors died in service, many suffered life-changing injuries. During the course of his career and fighting Nelson was to lose the sight in his right eye and later lose his right arm, then finally his life itself.

He was well known for ignoring orders when it suited him, which resulted in some of his greatest victories. When ordered to cease action at the Battle of Copenhagen, he put his telescope to his blind eye, later explaining he had not seen the signal.

Apart from his fame for defeating Napoleon, firstly at the Battle of the Nile in 1798, he is also famous for his affair with Lady Emma Hamilton. Both were already married, stayed married to their respective partners, and together bore a daughter, Horatia.
He was again to defeat Napoleon at the Battle of Trafalgar, which saved Britain from invasion. Here he gave his famous order, "England expects

that every man will do his duty." A few hours later a French sniper fatally wounded him. Rather than burial at sea, as would happen to a lesser person, his body was preserved in Brandy so it could be returned to England for a state funeral.

Could it have been Napoleon Brandy?

Some time earlier his cry on boarding the San Joseph, "Victory or Westminster Abbey," was an ironic epitaph as of course he died achieving his victory at Trafalgar on his flagship Victory. You could almost say he should have cried "Victory and Westminster Abbey," except he was buried in St Paul's Cathedral. Some wags state his body will be preserved forever having been pickled in brandy.

Westminster Abbey

He is remembered by his famous statue on the enormous column at the location since named Trafalgar Square. The square originally carried the name "Charing Cross" which remains the name of the nearby major rail terminus. The square was to have been named "King William the Fourth's Square." William the Fourth Street is very close to Trafalgar Square.

During the Second World War, one of Britain's most important battleships was named the Nelson. U-boat ace Otto Kretschmer, unusually for a U-Boat commander, survived the war (he was subsequently captured). Even more unusually, he had a sense of humour. On one patrol at night he saw through his periscope what he thought was a ship and put two torpedoes into it. It turned out to be a rock jutting out of the sea. The German word for rock is Felson, so Kretschmer radioed back (in German, of course), "Felson torpedoed but not sunk."

Goebbels and the German Propaganda Ministry got hold of this, but not surprisingly misread as, "Nelson torpedoed but not sunk." They promptly announced this to the world. Rather unusually, as warship positions were usually kept secret, the British Propaganda Ministry countered with something along the lines of, "How could he have torpedoed a ship from several thousand miles away?"

Apparently, the head of the U-Boat arm, Admiral Karl Doenitz also had a sense of humour. On receiving Kretschmer's report he laughed and said to him, "So you sank a rock?"

Doenitz briefly took over as Fuhrer in May 1945 following Hitler's suicide.

There is a well-known picture representing Nelson receiving the Spanish officers' swords on the quarterdeck of the San Joseph, and William Fearing, one of his bargemen, receiving them and putting them under his arm. John Sykes was his coxswain when he was in command of the inner squadron blockading Cadiz. The Spanish gunboats having annoyed him, he resolved to attack them with boats in the night. So in they pulled, Nelson's barge with ten men --Captain Freemantle and Jack were with them -- when suddenly they found themselves alongside a Spanish launch with twenty-six men or more. It was a desperate fight. Sykes and Nelson were in the thickest of the fray. Blow after blow aimed at Nelson was warded off by him until his arm was laid open, and even after that be sprang forward, and his head received the blow intended for his chief. Eighteen Spaniards were killed, and the rest of them, mostly wounded, surrendered, and we towed off the launch. This was the kind of enthusiasm that Nelson kindled in his men.

He went to sea at twelve years of age, first upon an Arctic voyage, when, being missed one day, he was discovered on an iceberg attempting to get at a large Polar bear. A boat was sent for him, and he was brought back and reprimanded. He served actively as a lieutenant, and at twenty-two was made a Post-Captain, and by some called," Our Boy Captain." He was appointed to command the Agamemnon, one of the most wretched sailors among all the seventy-fours, though in reality she was only a sixty-four, yet in her he performed prodigies of valour, so that his ship was feared and respected. The crew, consisting mostly of Norfolk men, were ennobled by the term of "Brave Agamemnons." He was, before his death, the hero of one hundred and twenty-seven fights. So much for this little digression by the way, which must be excused, as I afterwards served under him in the Vanguard.

The admirals having sent carpenters to examine us, reported that we were fit for sea, when we immediately refitted to cruise off Cadiz again, to look after the Spaniards with the fleet. Then we saw them lying snugly inside like a lot of cowards, being double our number, and afraid to come out. Whilst off Cadiz, sometimes at anchor, sometimes cruising about, we had very bad usage, which caused a great number of our ship's company to prepare to mutiny. But being found out by a ship's corporal, who was in the sick bay, he went aft over the poop into the captain's cabin and gave information. The captain prepared immediately, and quietly finding out the ringleaders secured them, one of whom, named Taylor, turned king's evidence. The four next to him were tried the next day, found guilty, and executed the day after. It was reported that Sir John Jervis was so strict, that he would not have forgiven his own father if he had found him amongst the mutineers. The mutiny now being at the Nore and other seaports in England made him act promptly and with decision. A little while after this, the boatswain of the Emerald frigate was executed for a few trifling words wrongly construed.

We having lost two anchors whilst lying here, the admiral sent us to Lagos Bay to pick up some the Spaniards left behind, when they wanted to get out of our way in such a hurry, that they cut their cables and ran. We arrived at the anchorage, and fished up two bower anchors, three kedges, and several cables, and returned to the fleet. Whilst we were away an American ship passed through the fleet, reporting that he saw us thirty leagues to the westward of Cape St. Vincent, bound for England, the crew having mutinied, which, when we arrived, was found to be false.

The end of August we received orders to go to Lisbon, to take the four Spanish prizes to England. Parted from the fleet in the night, the next day were joined by the Britannia, the Seahorse frigate having passed us with Nelson on board, bound for England, he having lost his arm at Teneriffe in an unsuccessful night attack, being sent by Admiral Sir John Jervis to cut out a rich Manilla galleon which lay in the harbour of Santa Cruz. His squadron consisted of four ships of the line, three frigates, and the Fox cutter. In the darkness the boats missed each other, and did not land together at the Mole,

However Nelson would not turn back, but drawing his sword sprang on shore, when he received a musket-ball through his arm, and he fell back into the arms of his step-son, Lieutenant Nisbet, who immediately stopped the flow of blood by tying his silk handkerchief tightly round his arm above, and a sailor made him a sling of part of his shirt. He was taken on board, where it was found necessary to amputate the arm. Our loss in men and officers was two hundred and fifty killed and wounded. Captain Trowbridge made good his landing, and took command of all that were left; gallantly succeeded in taking the town, drew his men up in the principal square, and when summoned to surrender by the governor, declared that if they did not let him march unmolested to his boats, he would burn the town, and then cut his way through them. The Spanish governor, not wishing the town burnt, gave him what he asked for, and quietly allowed him to march to his boats and embark for the ships. When we were off Cape St. Vincent the Victory, 100, joined us, and arriving at Lisbon we got the prizes ready, and sailed for England. When in the Channel, off Plymouth, had a heavy gale, which caused us to run into Torbay for shelter; but the wind changing we sailed, and saw the prizes safely inside the Eddystone Lighthouse, under the charge of the master attendant of Plymouth dockyard.

We then sailed for Spithead, arrived there, and waited there three days in quarantine, then received orders to convoy a fleet of merchant ships, which had been waiting at Spithead, to the eastward, that is, through the Downs and up the Thames; but, we had got no farther than St. Helen's Point, Isle of Wight, when orders came to return to the anchorage at Spithead, for news had arrived that the Dutch fleet was out, the French having overrun Holland, and got the Dutch fleet under their power. We remained three days, when the news arrived that Admiral Duncan had defeated the Dutch, and had taken several ships of the line.

Quarantine

In the days of sail, disease, common with the bad diet and unsanitary conditions at the time, could not be suppressed through the use of vaccines. Very few had been developed at that stage. Surprisingly the smallpox vaccine was developed as long ago as 1796. The only way to slow the spread of disease following an outbreak was by quarantining those affected, and those serving with the victims.

In some cases, crews were placed on ships specifically designated as quarantine ships, otherwise knows as lazarettos, until the risk had passed. One famous such ship was named the Dreadnought. A later ship carrying that name, launched in 1906, was the first of the type of battleship termed "Dreadnoughts." It could be argued that she was the mother of all future battleships. She represented a massive leap forward in technology, sporting 10 twelve-inch guns and a top speed of 21 knots. She was the first battleship with steam turbine engines. She was also the first and only battleship that ever sank a submarine (the general intention was the other way round) when she rammed the German Submarine U29 at the Battle of Jutland.

The term lazaretto or lazaret, which can also cover a shore-based building, comes from the name of Lazarus the Beggar, as cured by Jesus in the Gospel according to Luke.

A famous example of the quarantine system breaking down occurred in 1845 when after HMS Éclair left Sierra Leone in Western Africa, a large proportion of her crew started dieing from Yellow Fever. The ship put into Boa Vista, Cape Verde Islands where they were allowed ashore as they claimed they didn't have yellow fever and they weren't contagious. Subsequently a third of the island's population died.

Admiral Duncan

We then proceeded to Sheerness with our convoy. When off the North Foreland were joined by the Victory, 100, for Chatham, likewise to be laid up in ordinary. We arrived at Sheerness; got out our guns, stores, powder, etc. Whilst laying here the English fleet, under Admiral Duncan, arrived with the Dutch prizes. The news spread like wildfire, and for several days the harbour was covered with boats crowded with people to see them. After this we proceeded to Chatham, dismantled the ships, and returned everything to the dockyard. There we lay, having a rest after our toils and hardships; not only rough weather, but, sometimes only half fed, and that of a very inferior kind of biscuits so eaten by weevils that we could hold them up and nearly blow them away with our breath, the salt beef and pork so hard that we called it junk, a name given by sailors to pieces of old rope or cable. We were now enjoying ourselves, oftentimes neither wisely nor well, not expecting that it would last long. I entered the St. George February 8th, 1793, and remained in her until March 4th, 1798, upwards of five years' hard and rough service, first as an ordinary, and then as an able seaman, but gaining a knowledge and experience invaluable to a sailor.

Weevils

At the time Mr Shirley Senior was at sea, there were often so many weevils, maggots, cockroaches and other bugs living in the sailors' food whilst in warmer climates that they preferred to eat in the dark. Out of site, out of mind.

The bread they ate, hard tack, was baked 3 times to make it completely dry. In cooler climates (such as in British waters most of the time) it could last for up to five years. However, in hot, humid climates the hard tack would rehydrate, allowing insects to breed quickly.

In actual fact, most of the smaller bugs then referred to as weevils were bread beetles, a relative of the woodworm.

Fortunately, by this time, although unappetising, the diet was reasonably healthy. The Scottish Royal Navy surgeon James Lind had proved scurvy (severe vitamin C deficiency) could be cured by eating fruit. It took some time to act upon his findings, but by the 1790s Royal Navy ships were the first to carry lemons, immediately controlling the problem. Until then, more British sailors died of scurvy than enemy action.

CHAPTER II. 1798 - 1837

Our rest soon terminated. In March 1798 we were all called into active service again. One hundred and fifty of our crew were drafted to the Vanguard, 74, fitting at the Nore to be the flagship of Rear-Admiral Nelson, and the rest of our crew to other ships. I was sent to the Vanguard. Paid our wages, and sailed to Spithead. We anchored near the wreck of the Royal George, which had been sunk about sixteen years, and upwards of nine hundred of her crew being drowned.

Nelson

Whilst on the passage I received a slight hurt, for which our excellent doctor sent me to Haslar Hospital. On the day the ship unmoored the captain sent for me and his coxswain. Admiral Nelson hoisted his flag, and we sailed for Cadiz. Arrived there, were sent by the Commander-in-Chief to cruise off Cadiz and watch the French fleet, our squadron consisting of three sail of the line, two frigates, and one corvette. On May 21st our watching them was put to an end, for we had to watch ourselves. In a heavy gale of wind at 1 a.m. our main and mizzen topmast went over the side, and at 4 a.m. our foremast went into two pieces on the forecastle, the top on the larboard and the yard on the starboard side. There we lay with our hatches battened down, the ship's company only having bread and cheese for three clays, the provisions on the lower deck being spoiled. At last, clearing our deck, we got her before the wind. We had parted with the frigates and corvette in the gale; made signal for the Alexander to take us in tow; steered for St. Pierre's Bay, but nearly got on the rocks in a cairn. A breeze, however, springing up we got safely in, in company and with the help of the Orion. Fitted the ship with a jury foremast. Whilst refitting here we heard that the French fleet had passed, bound for Egypt. (They might have taken us all.) As soon as ready we sailed for Toulon, and fell in with ten sail of the line, one fifty, and one brig, come to reinforce us. But where were the frigates--Alas! Where? --So very essential to the operation of a fleet which has to hunt out an enemy? There were none. We then made sail after the French, passed up between Elba and Corsica, hence to Naples; had communication with the shore, but no news of the French. What Nelson wanted now was frigates to cruise in different directions to gather up intelligence. He called them the eyes of the fleet, the scouts, who were to be here, there, and everywhere. As it was, he was obliged to keep his fleet of seventy-fours together, but being without frigates the French fleet escaped him. Sailing through the Faro-de Messina, where we were cheered by thousands of people on shore and in boats, past Candia, thence to Alexandria, but no French, arriving at Aboukir Bay June 28th, and afterwards found that we must have passed through or near them, but were not seen, it being foggy. They arrived on July 1st, three days after us. Not getting any clue of them, sailed immediately to Syracuse to get eater and beef, being on short allowance of provisions excepting wine. There we heard that the French had taken Malta and sailed for Alexandria. We sailed after them again, and when off Candia heard from a brig (which the Culloden took in tow) that the French fleet were at anchor in Aboukir Bay, about twenty miles eastward of Alexandria.

Sail of the Line

The Ship (or Sail) of the Line was the most common type of fighting ship at the time. The concept was simple, to put as many guns as possible of the highest possible calibre on each ship. As ships were dependent on wind power, little tactical manoeuvring was possible, so opposing ships would simply sail along, side by side, pumping as many canon balls into each other as they could. Hence the navy with the largest, most numerous, most powerful ships (i.e. generally the Royal Navy) would win the battle.

Although much bigger ships existed, the most common size of Ship of the Line was the 74-gun.

Once engines were added to some ships in the 1840s, then later iron cladding, finally fully metal ships, the battleship became the descendent of the "line of battle ship" simply by abbreviating the name.

On August 1st, by the day of the month but the second by the log-book, about two o'clock in the afternoon, saw the enemy moored in line of battle in the form of half a moon near the shore. We made signal for the Culloden to cast off the brig. She and three other ships having taken a stretch across to Alexandria to look into the harbour, were now coming across to join us, so as to form our line of battle, the Culloden being eight miles astern. Soon after she grounded upon a shoal, which the others who were following in her wake avoided. But she remained on the shoal, and was attended by the La Mutine brig (Captain Hardy), to render her any assistance she might require.

The French fleet was commanded by the brave Admiral Brueys, who had cleverly moored them in the shape of half a moon, sails all furled, and cleared for action, each ship having two anchors out at the head, and two at the stern, so as easily to alter their position if required. There were sands and shallows between him and the shore. He naturally thought that none would attempt to get between him and the shoals; besides, there were forts on the shore.

But Nelson, who was a skilful pilot, thought that if there was room enough for them to swing round, there would be for him to get inside if carefully done. He formed his plans, and they were at once carried out. We were ready for action, with our cables out of the sternposts, bent to the anchors forward to let go when near enough the enemy, so as to prevent his cutting us to pieces in swinging round.

Captain Hardy

Sir Thomas Hardy, first Baronet, was the famous commander to whom it is believed that Nelson implored him to "kiss me, Hardy," as Nelson lay dieing at the Battle of Trafalgar.

Hardy's Pub, Trafalgar Road, Greenwich, London

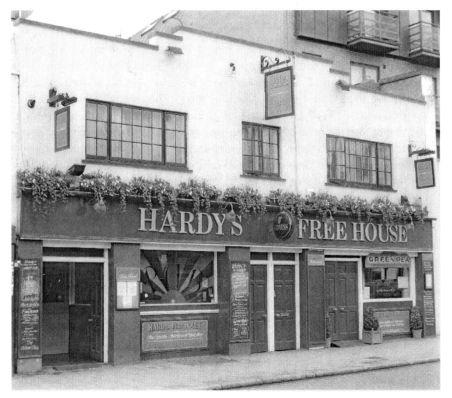

The name of this pub is nothing to do with Captain Hardy

Born in 1769, he first joined the Royal Navy at the age of 12, serving on HMS Helena. After a short time onboard, he attended school for 3 years before joining the merchant navy. He rejoined the Royal Navy in 1790.

By 1796 Hardy had reached the rank of lieutenant, serving initially under Captain Cockburn, when the commander of the squadron to which it was attached, Captain Nelson, transferred his flag there.

That same year, Hardy was captured by the Spanish, but was released thanks to an exchange of prisoners.

In 1798 Hardy himself captured (La) Mutine and as a reward Admiral Jervis promoted him Commander and gave him the Mutine's captaincy. He was promoted again to Captain the same year, and appointed as Flag Captain to Nelson on HMS Vanguard.

Hardy and Nelson got along very well, having similar outlooks to important matters such as discipline. This gave Nelson the freedom to concentrate wholly on commanding the squadron while Hardy handled the flagship itself.

Hardy was transferred away from Nelson the next year, but in 1801 he rejoined him as flag captain of HMS San Josef, then to HMS St George, before rejoining Nelson again on HMS Elephant.

He parted from Nelson yet again to command HMS Isis before rejoining him in 1803, firstly on HMS Amphion, then on HMS Victory again as Flag Captain. By this time Nelson was Commander in Chief.

Nelson was mortally wounded by a French sniper at the Battle of Trafalgar, on the 21st October 1805. He was shot through the spine.

Hardy had ably assisted Nelson at his side throughout the battle. Both walked in full view of snipers, so it is unsurprising that one of them took a fatal bullet. Hardy was by Nelson's side as he was carried below decks to die. Nelson even stopped those carrying him on the way so he could give advice to one of his sailors.

There is no absolute proof that Nelson uttered the instruction, "kiss me, Hardy," and if he did, the exact words are unsure. In the heat of battle, the words of a dieing man can be misidentified, but all three of the eyewitnesses believe this is the gist of what he said.

Admiral Hardy Pub, College Approach, Greenwich, London

This one is named after Captain / Admiral Hardy

In recognition of his role at the Battle of Trafalgar, he was created a Baronet. He had not reached the rank of Admiral by the end of his service (attaining the rank of Vice Admiral), but in 1830 was made First Sea Lord. There is no single commander of the Royal Navy, but the First Sea Lord and First Lord of the Admiralty are the two persons who are nearest to being overall commander. A board, the Board of the Admiralty, heads the Royal Navy, hence this non-unified command structure.

Hardy died in 1839 and is buried in the grounds of Greenwich Hospital.

At thirty-five minutes past 6 p.m., the sun half below the horizon, a fine clear night, a moderate breeze, we commenced the action. The enemy having fired much at us before we were in gunshot, Nelson's plans were skilfully carried out, several ships getting inside, and the rest of the ships outside of the half moon, thus putting the rear and centre between two fires. Thus they were soon overpowered and destroyed. The van could not easily leave their places, the sails all being furled; they were either unable, or without orders to assist their consorts. Nelson, by getting inside, took the enemy somewhat by surprise; for in all probability the guns on that side of the ship were not in position for action, they expecting the attack to be made on the seaward side only, our ship, the Vanguard, taking two broadsides from the two French ships and returning them with interest, the fire of the English being more vigorous than the French. The Vanguard anchored near the Spartiate within half pistol shot, nailing the colours to each mast, opening a tremendous fire, under cover of which four ships passed us, and anchored opposite. The next four French ships engaged them in close fight; they were the Minotaur, Bellerophon, Defence, and Majestic, 74's.

Nelson's Column, Trafalgar Square. London

So hot was the French fire on the Vanguard that in a few minutes every man at the six foremost guns was either killed or wounded, and three times they had to be re-manned. If the French fire was destructive ours was more so, for within a quarter of an hour of the commencement, the two first French ships were dismasted, and by half-past nine six ships of the enemy had struck their colours. Nelson received a wound, which was at first thought fatal; probably he thought so himself. A langridge shot stripped the skin from his forehead, which, falling over his remaining eye, put him in darkness. The blood flowing freely was alarming at first, but was soon found not to be serious; then he insisted on taking his turn under the doctor's hands. On being dressed and bandaged up, an alarm of the French admiral's ship L'Orient being on fire. Nelson hearing it, slipped out of the cockpit, and came on deck. I was, with several others, standing under the poop gazing at the grand but awful sight, when the admiral passed us going into his cabin. He stopped to say, "You see, my men, what it is to be in an undisciplined ship." He was a disciplinarian, and took this opportunity of showing its value. Soon after she blew up with an awful explosion, portions of her timber falling all around. It is said she had on board half a million of specie, the plunder of Malta, and many other valuables; the clergy of the cathedral only saving their silver railings round the altar by painting them black. Nelson humanely ordered the boats to put out, and they succeeded in saving about seventy lives. The fire of the ships was only desultory after this the whole of the night. At daybreak we found that ten sail of the line and ten frigates were in our possession. During an action like this the sailors and officers that are between decks cannot see much of the general fight, it is rapid firing into each other, but I was quartered at an 18-pounder carronade on the poop, which was early disabled; but the signal midshipman being killed early in the action, I had to assist the flag-lieutenant with the signals. He ordered me to look after the Culloden, which was aground on a shoal during the action; thus we were a ship short as well as the La Mutine brig. I reported her swinging off to Captain Berry. Just before the action commenced I pulled off everything but my trousers, took my two watches out of my fobs or watch-pockets, and rolling them up in my shirt put them behind the flagstaff, saying to myself, "Well, if I am killed, here is a prize for some of the survivors." Soon after daylight, three sail of the line and two frigates, all that was left of the entire French fleet, got under weigh to get out of the bay and escape, one of which, the Timoleon, 80, whose foremast was injured, being unable to bear the pressure of the sail, went on one side, and being thus disabled, to prevent us taking her, she was run on shore and set on fire. The others, four in number, namely, Guillaume Tell, 80, Generaux, 80, and two frigates, escaped. These ships formed the van, and were comparatively little injured in the battle. It is said that the Zealous (Captain Hood), which was the only ship in a condition to pursue them, owed it to the captain bringing her round into an angular position, so as to escape most of the broadside fire of the two French ships, whilst he was most destructive by being more raking; and had they shifted their position it would have brought them into receiving the raking fire of the next ship. Captain Hood immediately sailed out of the bay after them, but having no other ship in the condition to support her, Nelson reluctantly signalled him to return; for had he followed them well out of the bay they would in all probability have returned, closed around, and overpowered him.

The battle of the Nile marked an epoch in our navy. It was the resurrection of the days of Cromwell, when Admiral Blake showed them unmistakably the stuff that British sailors were made of, never knowing when they were beaten if properly led and treated. In this battle our ships were only 74's, and were not near so powerful as the French 80's, and the L'Orient was a powerful three-decker, carrying 130 guns. Though the fleets were nearly equal in number of ships, the men and guns were greatly in favour of the French, and we were deprived of the service of the Culloden, which* grounded on a shoal. The victory was so complete in the annihilation of their fleet, that our navy became a terror to all nations. Of the thirteen line of battle ships when the action commenced we took nine, two were burned, and two escaped, and out of four frigates, one burnt, one sunk, and two escaped. The French lost upwards of three thousand one hundred killed and wounded. On our side Captain Westcott was the only commanding officer killed, and between eight and nine hundred killed and wounded.

After the close of the action an order was issued that all on board every ship should thank God for giving us the victory. How many hearty thanksgivings were offered that day by the survivors! You may imagine the awe and solemn stillness--not a word spoken; the silence was only broken by the chaplain commencing the prayer. The Egyptians and Arabs wondered at the silence, and the French officers who were prisoners on board, and mostly infidels, listened with respect. When Napoleon heard of the loss of his fleet he broke the news to his officers at the breakfast table thus," Well, gentlemen, how do you like Egypt? "

Their reply generally was "Very well," to which he replied, "I am very glad you do, for Nelson has taken and destroyed our fleet, and there are no means of getting back to France."

We laid in the bay some time, refitting and getting six of the French line of battle ships ready to send to England, the other four being so shattered that they were destroyed. Captain Berry, afterwards Sir Edward Berry, sent for me to say that Lieutenant Capel recommended me for promotion for good conduct during the action, therefore he had rated me a quartermaster's mate, and dated it two months back, so as to give me a greater share of prize money. He then sailed for England in the Leander, 50, with official despatches from Nelson to the Admiralty, giving an account of the battle of the Nile and the glorious victory, which resulted in the almost total destruction of the French fleet. Captain Hardy, of the La Mutine brig, succeeded Captain Berry, and we (the Vanguard) sailed in company with the Culloden and Alexander, which had occasionally to tow the Culloden to Naples. Having sent the six prizes to England with six English ships, we left the rest to cruise off the Egyptian coast and watch the French. We passed through the Faro de Messina. When off Stromboli we lost our jury foremast in a white squall, and signalled to the Thalia frigate to take us in tow. When we arrived at the Bay of Naples Sir William and Lady Hamilton came on board to congratulate the admiral on his success. When we anchored, the bay was covered with boats crowded with people, who cheered us heartily. The admiral went on shore with them, and was enthusiastically received by tens of thousands of people. We were now very busy refilling the ship, repairing the foremast, and other damages received in the white squall. These finished, we sailed with troops for Leghorn, landed them, and returned to Naples. Whilst there the French armies had overrun Italy very rapidly, the Neapolitan soldiers making scarcely a show of fighting, but invariably retreating when the French were in sight. Ferdinand, their king, always remembered this; for his minister, a few years after this, recommended a cuirass for the cavalry after the French fashion. The king, with it smile, asked him where it was to he worn, He replied on the breast, to protect the heart, lungs, and vital parts. "Ali," said the king, "it is of no use to Neapolitan soldiers, for they want plates to their backs."

Nelson, Trafalgar Square, London

Sir William and Lady Hamilton

Horatio Nelson and Emma Hamilton's affair was one of the most famous in history.

Despite the morally correct attitude associated with the Victorian era, soon to commence, Emma's life demonstrates that when it comes to sex, nothing is new. Born Amy Lyon, but preferring to be known as Emma Hart, from the age of 12 she was working as a nursemaid for composer Thomas Linley (the "English Mozart"). At about age 16 she went to live at a brothel.

After this she was noted as being an attendant in the Temple of Health and Hymen, whose owner gave lectures on procreation and allowed couples to use his "Great Celestial State Bed" for £50 a night where "perfect babies could be created."

Next she moved to the property of Sir Harry Featherstonehaugh where it was alleged she danced naked on his dining table to entertain his friends (the first Table Dancer, perhaps?). It was also alleged she had a child with him, named Emma Carew.

At this time she met the Hon. Charles Greville, nephew of her later husband Sir William Hamilton. Greville commissioned artist George Romney to produce a series of paintings of her. He also made sketches, apparently including nude ones. She lived with him until he became bored with her, deciding he wanted the Hon. Henrietta Willougby instead. So he introduced Emma to his uncle, stating in a letter, "a cleaner, sweeter bed-fellow did not exist."

Emma agreed with Greville that she should go to Naples to stay with Sir William for six months, after which he would return to collect her. He never did. However, fortunately Sir William was completely smitten with Emma. She gradually accepted his attentions and after returning to England in 1791 they were married. This was also the same year she met Nelson for the first time. Over several meetings through an extended period, they fell in love, until in 1801 their daughter Horatia was born. Nelson left his wife; then two years later Sir William died leaving Emma a respectable income. Nelson also was to die just two years after this. Emma was not allowed to attend his funeral.

In a way that would be unusual even today, Emma and Nelson had carried on their affair whilst she was living with Hamilton. It is not known for sure if he knew, but surely he did, and apparently was happy to allow it. He even was friends with Nelson. Clearly once Emma became pregnant he had to have known what was happening (unless she was sleeping with both of them – probably not, he being a sugar daddy).

Society however was unwilling to accept the affair. Nelson and Hamilton were both recalled from Naples in disgust and Emma was rejected by society. Typically of the sexism so prevalent, Nelson and Hamilton were forgiven. Emma never was.

As the French were rapidly nearing Naples, Nelson one night suddenly ordered all the boats of the fleet to be got ready, flannel served out, and the oars of the boats bound round with it so as to muffle them, enabling them to pull without any noise, which they did. The only sound was their dipping the oars in water; not a word was spoken, Nelson having ordered perfect silence.

At length they arrived at the back of the palace. Nelson ascended the steps and knocked at the door. This was the only sound heard. A man looked over the balcony on the roof, and disappeared. Presently the door opened, and he went in. In a short time it was opened again, and Nelson, the king and queen, princes and princesses, members of the court, Sir William and Lady Hamilton, and servants, with all their treasures and valuables, very quietly got in the boats, and at a given signal silently left the shore. Soon they and their treasures were safely on board the fleet, no one in Naples knowing anything about it. However, the news soon spread, that the king and the court were all safely on board the British fleet and the bay was soon covered with boats coming with deputation` from all classes in Naples, to ask him to return and put himself at their head, and they would shed the last drop of blood they had left in their veins for him and his family. Notwithstanding all their tears and entreaties he was afraid to trust himself with them. The Lazzaroni, or roughs of the population, rose en mass when the French entered Naples, and made a most determined resistance. Though without a leader, or any organised means of defence, they did more than the whole of the Neapolitan army in stopping their onward march.

Nelson sailed with the fleet for Palermo, so as to land them all in Sicily, where they would he quite safe, the French being unable to follow them, Nelson holding command of the sea.

On the voyage we were caught in it white squall. The Vanguard lost her topsails, and was much afraid of losing her masts. The youngest child of the royal family died. We landed the whole at the Mole at Palermo, and laid there for a short time, during which we had it grand hall on board, the ship's leek being gaily fitted with flags. The king gave a cask of dollars to be distributed amongst the crew, and also three days' holiday at his request. It is supposed that we brought on board from Naples more than a million of money, which the French would have liked very much to have fingered.

During the holiday large numbers of our crews had liberty on shore at Palermo. Often they strolled a great many miles out, sometimes getting noisy and troublesome by using the wine-shops; and in those unsettled times some of the little fishing towns and villages contained a very rough population, not particularly honest. When on shore, or going any distance inland or along the coast. I invariably carried a hanger (a kind of broadsword), which made me respected. One day there was a large number on shore from the various ships of the fleet. Getting towards evening they were rather noisy and mischievous. I cautioned them about it, but only got abuse for my interference; so on they went, but were stopped about a mile from Palermo by the horse soldiers, who told them that they would not be allowed to enter the city in that disorderly state. Where was their officer? Some of them came running back to me to say I must be their officer, for my sword would be a badge of my office. With a short reprimand they fell in, and marched up to the main body, when the officer of the horse soldiers handed them over to me, and we marched into the city, thence to our boats at the hole pretty orderly, considering, all things, as they numbered some hundreds.

We had several cruises. In the summer of 1799, hearing that a French fleet was out from Brest, Nelson got the whole fleet together, and, arriving at Naples, moored them in line of battle, landed sailors and marines, and bombarded the castle of St. Elmo, then held by the French. Captain Trowbridge commanded the attacking forces, opening his first batteries within five hundred yards, and soon a second at two hundred yards. The French soon capitulated, and were expelled from Naples. Engineer officers having found limit, with the mode of attack and approaches, Nelson replied, "You would approach with your works in the old zigzag way, but Mr. Trowbridge went straight on, for none but a sailor would think of opening his first batteries at five hundred yards and his second at two." Whilst lying here, Prince Caraccioli, a Neapolitan admiral, was tried and found guilty--the king being on the trial--although it was under compulsion that he joined the French, therefore he should have been dealt leniently with. However, he was hanged at the yardarm of one of their own frigates. He was buried in the bay, his body being sewn up in a hammock or sack with shot in it to sink if to the bottom. But I suppose that it was clumsily clone, for the shot came out and the body rose, and the admiral came up head and shoulders above the water, and was seen by a Neapolitan fisherman, who was doubtless frightened out of his wits, and hastened to bring the astounding intelligence that the admiral was out in the hay. A boat was sent accordingly to sink the body in a proper manner. Nelson was much blamed for taking part in his trial.

The French fleet were not in these seas. We sailed with the king and Lord Nelson to Palermo. While we were there the Foudroyant, 80, came from England, as a new flagship, and Nelson shifted to her with all his followers, of whom I was one. Captain I tardy (afterwards his captain at Trafalgar), his lieutenants, and all the officers, quartermasters, and all who had risen to rank by merit, being men whom he could trust in the various posts that they occupied. When we first went on hoard we had nothing to do, and walked about like gentlemen, pointed at by the crew as "admiral's followers," sometimes with not a very polite prefix. Not many days elapsed before they were shifted on board the Vanguard, and we fell into our duties as usual.

Soon after we sailed for Gibraltar, but when off Minorca we fell in with a ship with Sir Edward Berry, our old captain, on board, who went to England after the battle of the Nile with Nelson's dispatches containing the report to the Admiralty of the victory, and the ships taken. He was made a baronet. We went into Mahon, and Sir Edward was reinstated in his old post, Nelson putting Hardy in command of the Courageaux, late French frigate. We then sailed for Palermo, the Queen Charlotte, a three-decker of 120 guns, going inside the Mole for the inspection of the royal family, who had never seen a three-decker before. Went from there to Malta, which was blockaded by our ships by sea, and besieged by the Maltese on land, the French only holding La Valetta, the town, harbour, and forts. We had scarcely taken up our position when news arrived that a French fleet was out from Toulon with stores, etc., for the relief of Malta. We parted with the admiral, and left Malta, sailing to look after them, and three days after, just before daylight, we heard a heavy firing, and fell in with them, being chased by the

Trafalgar Grove, Greenwich, London

Alexander, 74, Northumberland, 74, and Audacious, 74, the El-Cora brig being with us. A general action ensued, the French trying all they could to escape. A French frigate struck at ten o'clock, and about the middle of the afternoon the Genereaux, 80, which had escaped from the Nile, struck her colours, the admiral being killed by a cannon ball. She was sent to Syracuse with the Alexander and Northumberland, having left the Audacious, 74, and El Cora brig in company with the frigate. We sailed for Malta, and joined the admiral, who had hoisted his flag on board the Lion, 64, off Valetta; the Queen Charlotte, 120, parted company, went down the straits supposed for Leghorn. We afterwards sailed for Palermo with Nelson on board. After laying there for a short time, sailed again for Malta, leaving Nelson on shore. The afternoon we arrived Captain Dixon, of the Lion, 64, signalled to us to anchor and prepare for battle, as the French were expected out to run for Toulon about midnight. We came to an anchor, the lighthouse S.S.E. about six miles, having the Alexander between us and the eastern shore. At twelve o'clock we heard a great firing to the S.B., and saw a great many fireworks, but did not understand them. We immediately weighed anchor and hove to. At 2 a.m. a brig bailed us, and said that the French were out, and on the starboard tack. We then made all possible sail, with the wind blowing very fresh about S.S.E. At daybreak we discovered a large French man-of-war, Guillaume Tell, 80, standing for us with her main topmast gone. Immediately we shortened sail and cleared for action. I was on duty on the loop, my office being to con the ship; that is, to give orders to the man at the wheel steering, by calling out larboard, or starboard, etc. Our men were eager for the fray, but Sir

Edward Berry was anxious that they should not fire until we were nearer, and slung himself from the poop by an halyard on the quarterdeck, shouting, "Don't fire until I command." The consequences were that we received the French broadsides first, which brought down our foretopmast. We immediately replied, but it was not so effective, as we were put in some confusion by clearing away the, foretopmast. We continued the action for forty minutes, sometimes on one side, sometimes on the other within pistol shot, the Guillaume Tell making every effort to run into us, which was skilfully avoided. At last she was so much disabled, that, getting under our weather-bow, she lay there until dismasted, when she struck her colours, we having lost our foretop-mast and mizzen-mast, and It number of killed and wounded, I being wounded slightly in the right shoulder by a large splinter. As it blew rather fresh, an officer of the boat's crew was put on board to take charge of her.

Larboard

An earlier term for the port side of the ship (left hand side). Hence there was larboard and starboard. However, for steering instructions, the word "port" was always used to avoid dangerous misunderstanding between an order given for steer starboard or steer larboard.

The tradition of sailing on the left comes from the fact that most ships would dock on their left hand side. When ships had steering oars, these were generally kept on the right side, as of course people are more often right handed. By docking on the left, there was less chance of the steering oar being crushed between the ship and port side.

Travel by horse was also on the left in Europe. This was safer as by passing on the left, if attacked you could strike back with your sword in your right hand. However, Napoleon liked to leave his mark by changing established practices (and more significantly resisting the Vatican's direction to travel on the left), so the French rode on the right. As they invaded different countries in Europe they made the inhabitants switch to travel on the right. The tendency was for countries to not swap back once the French were expelled. Britain and Ireland were never invaded by Napoleon so never changed.

Austria was a notable exception, reverting to travel on the left after the French occupation ended. However, when Germany annexed Austria in the Anschluss of 1938, they made the Austrians (and soon after Czechoslovakia, which had been part of the Austro-Hungarian Empire) revert to travel on the right. This time the Austrians and Czechs did not change back.

Sweden drove on the left until one night in 1967 when overnight they swapped sides (they did of course have to prepare over an extended period before-hand). This was to aid their car industry by being able to export the same version of each model as the one sold at home.

In the case of North America, travelling on the right was chosen as the custom was that carriage drivers sat on the left to be able to use the horsewhip held in their right hands. As European carriages were typically smaller, whips were used more in North America.

Britain, most of its former empire, plus Japan (thanks to British influence) and some other countries drive on the left. This causes an ironic situation in China, where China drives on the right, but Hong Kong, formerly British Occupied but since reverted to China, drives on the left. When travelling between the two, drivers have to change to the other side even though they're not leaving their own country.

A larger proportion of the world's railways run on the left rather than the right, as many of them were British built.

She was taken in tow by the Penelope frigate, and we by the Lion, 64. The other ships returned to continue the blockade of Malta. The next morning the Lion left us to go to the assistance of the frigate, for it appears that she had the Guillaume Tell in tow, and none of the French crew had been removed, only the principal officers. A British officer and a few sailors were in nominal possession. A little before dawn, one of the crew of the watch on board of the frigate observed that the Guillaume Tell was getting nearer to them, called the attention of the officer of the watch, who thought he saw a number of the French crew in the forepart of the ship, had his suspicions aroused, ordered the hawser to be cast loose, and to let her shift for herself until daylight. She could not get away, as she was dismasted. He signalled the Lion to come up, the crew were removed, divided amongst the other ships, and an English navigating crew put on board, the French wounded only being left.

They had formed a well-laid plan, and were near carrying it out. They had secured the hawser by which they were towed to the capstan, and were heaving it into the ship, gradually drawing her closer. Their plan was to have got from the bowsprit and bows with a rush upon the frigate deck, and capture her by overpowering her crew, and sailing in her for Toulon, leaving the Guillaume Tell to shift for herself, but it was discovered just in time.

We proceeded to Syracuse, arrived and rigged a jury mast, sailed for Palermo, where we heard the sad news that the Queen Charlotte was burnt off the island of Gorgona, a great number of the crew being either burnt or drowned, Lord Keith being on shore at the time. We then sailed with Lord Nelson, as we must call him, Sir William Hamilton, his lady, with all luggage on board for Leghorn, who were going to

England overland. At Leghorn the last I saw of my chieftain, whom I little expected I should ever see again; as brave a man as ever trod the deck of an English man-of-war, and the enthusiasm with which he ever seemed to inspire his officers and men was incredible. We often have sung since

"The battle of the Nile

Was the foremost on the pile.

For British sailors fought like lions

At the mouth of the Nile."

A sailor was put in irons said to be drunk, and being ordered to strip and secured to a gun preparatory to being flogged, he made a final appeal to the captain, by declaring that "'pon his honour he was not drunk." "Honour," said the captain;" where did you get any honour?"

"On the glorious first of August, when I fought like a man," was the reply." Cast him loose; I must believe him. He will never sully that honour achieved under Nelson."

No sooner had we landed our chief than we received orders to proceed to Port Mahon, to fit for Lord Keith, having got new masts refitted, and Lord Keith hoisted his flag. We then sailed for Gibraltar, where we found several transports and troop-ships. Whilst there, Sir Edward Berry (who was going to England) asked me which I would prefer to be, a gunner or a boatswain, for I was not qualified to be a carpenter. I said, thanking him, that I would prefer to be a gunner. He then told me to hold myself in readiness, for he would see I had a gunner warrant. I waited a considerable time, then made inquiry, and found that my name had been erased, but by whom I knew not.

We sailed to Tetuan Bay several times and back; saw several battles between the Spanish gunboats and the Moors. A laughable incident occurred at this time. A large pig that was on board jumped overboard. The ship was hove to, and a boat lowered to capture him, but he swam very fast. Although they chased him five or six miles they could not gain on him, the popular notion being that if a pig swims very far, he will cut his throat with the stroke of his hoofs, but this one showed no signs of tiring or cutting his throat, and the boat's crew were reluctantly obliged to give up the chase, and the pig landed safely on a foreign shore in a state of freedom, but for how long we could not tell. At last we sailed to the west, made a feint of landing the troops, then got all snug on board again; sailed to Tetuan, thence to Malta, the expedition being in three divisions. Sailed from Malta in company with the Kent,

74, having on board Sir Ralph Abercromby, the Commander-in-Chief of the expedition, for Marmorice Bay, in Asia Minor, one of the most commodious harbours in the world, landlocked all round. In fine weather the troops were landed and exercised, once being interrupted by a terrible hailstorm, the hail being as large as small eggs; cut a number of the tents to pieces.

We then sailed to Rhodes, Lord Keith wishing to have communication with Sir W. Sidney Smith. When we arrived Sir Sidney came on board, and remained a considerable time with the admiral. It was Sir Sidney Smith that landed his sea-dogs and marines at Acre, and for more than two months resisted all the attempts that Napoleon Bonaparte made to storm it, although he had made a great breach in the walls. Each attempt to storm was repelled principally by the seamen led by Sir Sidney in person. At length he was obliged to raise the siege and retreat. The Druses and other chiefs were only waiting to see the result of the siege which side to join. Had Napoleon taken Acre and been joined by the mountaineers nothing could have stopped his march to Constantinople, but Sir Sidney and his brave sailors and marines effectually stopped him; his three line of battle ships prevented him from coming in reach of their cannon, so that he could only attack it on the land side. Unfortunately for him he sent his siege train and cannon by sea, but Sir Sidney captured the whole, and used them against him. If he approached too near the coast in his retreat he was harassed by the British gunboats, and when he turned inland the mountaineers cut off all his stragglers, they having joined the victorious party. Lord Keith doubtless felt that Sir Sidney could assist him with valuable advice. After the interview we sailed to Marmorice Bay. Immediately the fleet of troop-ships and transports, with the army on board, set sail for Aboukir Bay, escorted by the fleet; arrived there on the 4th of March; came to an anchor; the next day struck upon the wreck of the L'Orient, burnt at the battle of the Nile; got a stream cable to the Tigre, and hove in her wake let go the bower anchor, which kept us clear of the wreck. On the 7th, the wind being more moderate, we hove up and shifted our berth. On the 8th, it being fine weather, signal was made for the troops to embark in the boats of the fleet to land. We had seen the French making batteries on the sand-hills whilst prevented from landing by the rough weather. Standing on the poop of the Foudroyant I watched the boats full of red jackets in the stern and blue jackets rowing in the forepart, also the launches of the fleet with a gun at their bows rowing swiftly towards the beach, and then the French horse soldiers charged down the beach to the water. Instantly a streak of white smoke obscured everything; it was a discharge of grape shot from the guns in the bows of the launches, and musketry from the soldiers, that emptied most of the saddles. On the smoke clearing away, I saw a thin red line move up the beach, charging the French steadily forward, and driving them several miles inland.

We got the troops, guns, and stores all safely landed. Soon after two severe battles were fought, and the French were driven near Alexandria. When General Menou heard of our landing he pompously exclaimed, "I'll soon drive those beardless boys into the sea." But he found that if our soldiers were young, they were made of different stuff, and not so easily driven. He was, however, down sharp upon us, nearly surprising our troops, whose ammunition was short, it not being up to the front. The battle was desperate, but ended in the defeat of the French.

It is said that a French soldier was riding towards Sir Ralph Abercromby to cut him down. A Highlander who had exhausted his ball fired his ramrod through the advancing soldier and killed him. Soon after Sir Ralph was shot in the thigh, brought on board our ship, put into the admiral's cabin, where he died in a few days greatly lamented; was embalmed, and sent in the Flora frigate to Malta, we being sometimes near Alexandria, and sometimes in the bay, whilst here we had a new captain named Searle from the Determinee. It was an exchange, our captain, Bearer, going into the Determinee. At last we got the French out, of Egypt, the troops were ordered home, and on September 20th, 1801, before breakfast, Lieutenant Staines gave me a gunner's warrant, for the Tartarus bomb-ship at Alexandria. These bomb-ships carried two mortars on a large platform that threw shells. I saw one moored off Aboukir fort, and having got the range, that is, the exact distance, threw every shell into the fort, whilst the French kept up a heavy cannonade, but every shot fell short; not one reached the bombship. I was ordered to take a passage in the Seampavia gunboat to join my ship, which I did in three days. Whilst on board saw the crocodiles fast asleep floating down the Nile with the current. Lying here some time I saw Pompey's Pillar and Cleopatra's Needle. One feat of the sailors was to fly a kite across the Pillar, getting the string over the top, let the string go, so as for the kite to fall the other side, then fasten some ropes to the string, and pull them over until there were enough for them to climb up, enjoy the scene, and drink the king's health and confusion to his enemies.

Soon after sailed for Malta, thence to Cephalonia, Corfu, and Zante, where the currants grow that we are so fond of in our puddings, thence back again to Malta, parted with our anchors in a gale, and went on shore, but was speedily towed oil' by the Tigre, was hove down and repaired, then sailed for Gibraltar with two bomb tenders, but parted with them in the passage. On arrival found the Foudroyant with Lord Keith's flag and several other ships, took in water, and sailed for England.

Off Cadiz we fell in with some Portuguese men-of-war, who were on the lookout after some Algerines who had taken some of their merchant ships. In three weeks we arrived in the Downs, then sailed for Woolwich. On arriving at the Nore we hauled clown the yellow flag, having been in quarantine ever since we made Dungeness Light, laying three days in the boats, one day at Hythe, besides the Downs.

Algerine

The normal meaning of this word is an Algerian person. However, in those days it could also mean a pirate.

Arrived at Purfleet, put all my mortars, guns, and stores in a lighter for Woolwich. About three clays later followed, and returned lire remaining stores, was paid off, and the ship laid up in ordinary. I was obliged to go to Portsmouth to pass for a gunner (being only acting up to this time), which I did on board Admiral Millbank's ship on a Sunday, or I should have been discharged the service, twenty eight days being allowed after the ship was paid off.

Whilst we lay at the moorings the ship sprang a leak, and was hauled on the mud alongside the dockyard, so that what ran into her at high water ran out of her at low, when she was high and dry. I was now appointed gunner of the Matilda hospital ship, Lieutenant James, and a rum fellow he was. This concluded my adventures, extending over a period of nearly twelve years from a boy, to my receiving a gunner's warrant as an officer, and joining the Matilda on May 19th, 1803.

WHAT a change it seemed to be on "Home Service," the ship always moored in one place, --never a sail even unfurled, - monotonous in the extreme. My previous life had been so active, so restless, so full of incident, and now one so tame and dull. Before receiving my gunner's warrant, I had a circle of acquaintances among the quartermasters and petty officers, from whom I was now separated, and naturally thrown among the warrant officers of the ship; and as they only consisted of three, gunner, boatswain, and carpenter, it did not always happen they were suitable to each other, so I bought a Norway yawl about eighteen feet long, and ten feet beam, decked all over, with cabin for myself and it boy. I registered her to sail within a certain distance of the coast, and carry two fowling -pieces. So when I had two or three days to spare from my duties, I used to have a sail down to the Nore. Capital sea-boats were those yawls, never capsize, so broad on the beam, afraid of no rough weather, and carry any amount of sail. Many it night I have dropped my anchor and rode out a stiff gale. The boatmen on the Thames used to shake their heads when they saw me beating against a rising storm.

Fowling Piece

A light shotgun for shooting birds and small animals.

But hearing that the Cleopatra, a smart 32-gun frigate, was fitting out at Chatham, the gunner of which, being married, preferred it home life, a change was effected, and once more the prospect of active service was before me, and in a dashing frigate, the delight of a true seaman, although it was in different climes and scenes from which I had been used. She was appointed to the North American and West Indian station, and commissioned by Captain Sir I. Laurie. (*See further on below, to put into context the story of the capture of the Milan).

I joined on August 2nd, 1804, and when all was completed sailed for our destination, leaving my yawl in charge of a Thames waterman, little thinking I should not see the white cliffs of old England for ten years to come. Smart frigates were mostly employed as scouts to a squadron or a fleet, but we were mostly employed looking after French privateers, and protecting our merchantmen, as well as looking after their enemies. We were occupied, in conjunction with others, in operations against the French West India Islands, Guadeloupe, Martinique, etc., the harbours of which formed a refuge for privateers and ships of war. We were in the operations against Martinique which led to its capture, for which I received a bar to my medal. Once, when cruising off the island, we saw a number of ships in the harbour, the entrance of which was protected by forts on the high land, and I slung a gun, it long 12-pander, nearly perpendicular, according to the captain's order; and there being a good breeze we stood in toward the mouth of the harbour. The frigate lay well down, bringing the gun to an angle of forty-five. The forts opened fire. We sailed as near so as just to avoid it, then fired our gun, and the shot went over the forts into the harbour amongst the shipping, much, no doubt, to their astonishment.

We then put the ship about, satisfied with the experiment, and returned to our old cruising grounds, where we were successful in taking several prizes, and, putting at prize crew in each, sent them to Halifax or Bermuda, as we were obliged to put enough men on board to navigate them, and strong enough to overpower the crew should they attempt to rise and retake. We had to be careful that we 'made lawful captures, for if not condemned by the Admiralty Court, the captain and crew had to pay the cost of ship's detention, any damage to cargo, and the seamen's pay, together with any other loss the owners sustained.

After the capture of these prizes we were sailing from our old cruising grounds to Halifax to reship our prize crews, when the man at the masthead cried out, "A sail! A sail! "As she appeared to be steering for France we altered our course towards her. Upon nearing her we discovered that she was a large French frigate of 46 guns of heavier metal than ours, which were only long 12-pounders. She was called the Ville de Milan, and had a crew of five hundred, whereas ours, owing to the absence of prize crews, did not amount to scarcely two hundred.

However, the decks were cleared for action, and as soon as we were within gunshot it commenced, and continued for about three hours; but as we were severely damaged on that side of the ship, both the captain and the master thought it best to engage her on the other side. The master said, "As we are the best sailors let us drop astern, and sail up the other side."

"No," said the captain, "that will look as if we have had enough of it, and are running away. Let us sail ahead, cross her bows, and pass the ship, and wait for her on the other side." This advice was followed with the most disastrous consequences, for in crossing her bows a shot from the Milan killed the two men at the wheel, and cut the tiller ropes. She was unmanageable, sails flapping against the masts, before they could fix new ones. The French captain saw his opportunity; piped up the boarders, about two hundred and fifty men; ran his bowsprit right across the quarter-deck, and the boarders dropped on the deck of the Cleopatra like a swarm of bees, and we were instantly overpowered. Our colours were hauled down by the French, but rehoisted under the French tricolour. My post as gunner was in the magazine supplying the powder to my mate through a scupper, and he supplied the powder monkeys, as they were called. I felt the shock when the Milan ran into us, and said to my mate," Are they aboard of us?" His reply was, "I am afraid they are." Then I said, "I am afraid it is all over; our crew are so short." Immediately there was a great noise and confusion. It was a number of our crew had broken into the purser's storeroom, where he kept the clothes he supplied the sailors with, and were proceeding to rig themselves out in new suits before the French officers took charge of them. I was putting the magazine to rights, when two French officers came down to see it, and to take charge. In the French service the officers in charge of the powder, shot, and artillery were military, and their regulations are not so strict as ours. They were coming into the magazine with swords by their sides, when I called their attention politely to the rules of our service hanging up, by which no one was allowed to enter with any metal about him. My suit was of canvas with horn buttons, and canvas shoes. As soon as they understood they politely laid aside their accoutrements, saw all the arrangements, expressing their admiration. I then locked up and gave them the key. Being now a prisoner of war, I found I had only the doctor for a companion, who was left in charge of our wounded, and a few of the crew to help him. All the rest of the crew and the officers were removed on board the Cleopatra, and a prize captain and fifty men were sent to take charge of the Cleopatra, and navigate her.

Amongst the officers removed to the Milan was a midshipman named Provo Wallis, who first smelt powder in this action, having joined the navy the previous year. He said to a correspondent of the World (1888): "Nothing could be finer than the engagement of the little Cleopatra with her 12-pounders and the Great Ville de Milan, fought between Bermuda and the West Indies in February 1805, eight months previous to Trafalgar, and four months after I had joined the service. The action lasted for three hours. I soon got over my midshipman fright, and was as glad as the rest of them at not hauling clown our flag after all, but leaving the French to do it. We were only beaten by sheer superiority of size and numbers. We were not long prisoners; but the Cleopatra was soon retaken by the Leander, 50, as well as the Milan. Those were the clays when they were sailors not stokers." He still survives (1889), Sir Provo Wallis, (* See below, after the entry for Captain Laurie) an admiral of the fleet.

It was not till three or four days after our capture that I was permitted to come upon deck, and the sight brought tears to my eyes. Our tight little frigate looked a complete wreck, and all confusion some of the guns not properly secured, others in their wrong place. I asked permission of the prize captain to let me have a few men, and I would soon alter the appearance. He did. We soon made the deck look shipshape. In the collision we lost, our fore and mainmasts, only having a mizzenmast and two temporary rigged jury masts; these we made the more secure, and by the course we were steering were making the best of our way to France. After we had been captured about seven or eight days, being on deck, I saw the prize captain and several others looking earnestly at what appeared to be a sail. It rapidly gained on us, when he walked towards me, asking me what nation that ship belonged to?" Is it Espaniole?" said I. Half indignant he replied, "No; Espaniole in these seas?" When she approached considerably nearer, I was sure she was English, for there was the Union Jack at the foretop gallant-mast head. I went below to acquaint the doctor that deliverance was at hand, for an English man-of-war was rapidly approaching. The French captain, thinking I went below to tell the doctor, thought right, and ordered me on deck again. I observed that the Milan, which accommodated her sailing so as to keep us in company, now began to spread every stitch of canvas she could, evidently leaving us to our fate, thinking we should engage his attention for some time at least. Some time before she was in gunshot he placed his men at their quarters, cast loose the guns, run them in, and loaded them, preparing for action. The ship proved to be the Leander, 50. As soon as within range there was a puff of white smoke from her bows, and a shot struck the stump of the foremast to which the jury masts had been secured. The French, seeing the hopeless prospect of resistance, threw down their arms, and hastily went below. I instantly took charge, placed a sentinel where they disappeared, and went and Mauled down the tricolour that was flying over the English, and hoisted ours alone. She soon came up, and passing close hailed us with a speaking trumpet, "What ship) are you?" I replied, "The Cleopatra, captured by the Ville de Milan seven days since." The reply was, "Make sail, and follow me." The Leander never stopped, but stood after the Milan, and rapidly gained upon her, as she had a jury foremast and other severer damages inflicted by our 12-pounders before we were taken. I Watched with great interest the race; quickly was the distance lessened, and presently the white smoke rose from her bows, two reports were heard, and down came the French colours, judgment being shown, as the Leander, Captain Talbot, was the largest ship and perfect in every respect, whereas they were partly crippled.

Captain Basil Hall, who published more than sixty years since his "Fragments of Voyages and Travels," was a midshipman on board of the Leander, and in them he gives a graphic description from his point of view. He says there was a dense fog that morning, but it lay low, when the man at the masthead, who could see over the fog, cried," A sail," in a certain direction. The ship's course was altered, and the fog rapidly clearing he reported another sail --one a frigate with the French colours flying over the English, and the other a larger frigate with French colours only. The decks were cleared for action, men beat to quarters, and with all the canvas spread, she ploughed through it, occasionally sending some spray over the marines and wetting their pipe clay, to the intense delight of Jack, who had nothing on to spoil, and was eager to retrieve the disgrace of the English flag flying under the tricolour. What followed has been told, but he describes it as a glorious sight; the Leander towing the two ships into Halifax harbour with bands playing, firing of guns, and displays of flags, amid the cheers of the assembled population.

We immediately refitted, and soon our tight little frigate was as good as ever, and soon returning to our old cruising ground. During the time we were refitting the men were drafted mostly to other ships; but the officers and I preferred to stop, and so we sailed with nearly new crew and officers. The captain wished me to leave, as well as several after him, on being appointed to larger ships, but I steadily refused. At last one captain said he could not understand why I constantly refused to leave when I was repeatedly offered promotion with an increase of pay. I liked my ship, Dashing Cleopatra as she was called. Everything on board of her seemed clear to me; she was my home. Whilst I was in her we had seven captains, six carpenters, twelve boatswains, and two entire new ship's companies, between 1804 and 1813, a period of eight years and seven months.

Captain Sir I. Laurie.

In actual fact the commander of the Cleopatra at this time was Captain Sir Robert Laurie, 6th Baronet Maxwelton (as of the death of his father in 1804). The reason for the difference in first initial between history books and "There Go the Ships," is unknown.

The captain of the Leander at the time was John Talbot.

Captain Robert Laurie was court-martialled for the loss of the Cleopatra, but was honourably acquitted. He fought and wore down a superior enemy to the stage where on meeting any other British warship she would have been unable to defend herself, leading to the Leander being able easily to recover the Cleopatra and gain the much larger Ville de Milan as well.

The Ville de Milan was repaired and refitted and renamed HMS Milan. Captain Laurie was given her captaincy as reward. Later, in 1811 he was made captain of the bigger 74-gun HMS Ajax. The HMS Ajax launched in 1934 was to take part in the Battle of the River Plate and assist in the sinking of the far superior German Pocket Battleship Graf Spee.

During the battle the Cleopatra lost 22 killed and 36 wounded. Losses on the Ville de Milan are unknown but probably about 30 in total, but including the death of its captain, Captain Renaud.

Captain Laurie (born 1764) rose to the rank of Admiral of the White and held the title Knight Commander of the Order of the Bath. In another one of those interesting historical connections / coincidences, the captain of the (1934 launched) Ajax, Sir Charles Woodhouse, was also made Knight Commander of the Order of the Bath in return for his actions at the Battle of the River Plate in 1939.

Admiral Laurie died unmarried in 1848 meaning his Baronetcy died with him.

Sir Provo Wallis

Canadian Sir Provo Wallis was to live to the age of 100 (born 1791).

He "served" 96 years with the Royal Navy, thanks to his father convincing the captain of the HMS Oiseau to show him as a member of the crew of at the age of just four! He was listed on the ship's books as being an able seaman. At the age of five he "served" on HMS Prevoyante before transferring to HMS Asia from age 7 to 9. In 1800 he transferred to the Cleopatra, and was promoted to midshipman, with the advantage of several years seniority before he'd even started shaving! At age 13 he commenced actual duties, meaning as a midshipman he was commanding adult sailors.

In 1813, he temporarily made the rank of captain of the Shannon (aged 22) when as second lieutenant his captain was badly wounded and first lieutenant killed. During this "Battle of Boston Harbour" they captured the U.S.S. Chesapeake. 252 men on both sides were killed or injured. As reward, Wallis was promoted to Commander.

Wallis was substantively promoted to captain in 1819 (age 28) but did not receive his own ship until 1824 (HMS Niemen).

Promotion to rear admiral followed in 1851, then vice-admiral in 1857, finally admiral of the fleet in 1877. In his late 90's he was still on the active service list, so the Admiralty suggested he retire in case there was a call up. He refused, stating he was ready for a seagoing command if needed. He died in 1892 and was buried in the village churchyard of Funtingdon, near Portsmouth, England.

> And then there was another reason. We were mostly cruising by ourselves, a kind of a "free lance," our circle of officers small--there being but the captain, three lieutenants, master, and doctor, that were above me in rank, so we were more thrown together, and "less caste." I dined two and three times a week with one of my captains. Now in a 74-gun-ship which they wanted me to go with they had seven lieutenants, besides a captain of the marines, doctor, and master ranking above me, besides a crew of five hundred men. Then came the subject of prize money. It was quite clear that my share would not be one-fourth of what it would if I stopped in the Cleopatra. And again we were mostly by ourselves, and the prize was our own, whereas a 74 was mostly forming part of a squadron, and then every prize taken would have to be shared by the whole, and their opportunities would be considerably less, so that if I got a shilling in the 74 would likely get a pound in the frigate. And then the captain who pressed me for my

reasons said I was right, for I should only have an increase of pay of twenty pounds if I went into the larger ship.

Captain S. J. B. Pechell was captain of the Cleopatra twice, and was her last before she was laid up. I went with him into the San Domingo, a Spanish ship captured at Trafalgar, but commissioned into our service.

Captain S. J. B. Pechell

Apart from various times active in parliament as a Whig (the political party that later became the Liberals), Captain, later Rear-Admiral Samuel Pechell was active throughout his serving life in improving gunnery standards. This led to him being a personal friend of King William IV. He inherited the Pechell Baronetcy, but as he died childless this passed to his brother George. During his service he rose as far as being one of the Lords of the Admiralty.

Our course was pretty nearly the same, to and from the West Indies. In 1810 or 1811 we fell in with the Topiaze off Guadeloupe, and engaged her for forty minutes, when she struck. Several ships being in sight influenced the speedy surrender, the law being that every ship in sight shares in the prize money.

During my stay in the Cleopatra we had several narrow escapes. In the summer of 1805 we got on shore on the rocks at Bermuda, but got off again with some assistance. In 1809 we struck out the sternpost and a foot and a half of the steel end against a rock, and were obliged to keep the pumps going day and night till we arrived at port. In 1810 got on the Thrum Cap Shoal, at the entrance of Halifax Harbour, and remained there five hours, but were hove off by other ships. The Tribune was lost on this shoal, only being on it one hour, when she became a total wreck, and two hundred and fifty of her crew were drowned.

William IV Greenwich Park, London

I spoke of our having had twelve boatswains whilst I was in her. The question may he asked, Why so many boatswains? The sad truth has to be told. More than half of them had to be removed on account of drunkenness. One boatswain's mate had only been promoted a few hours; was sent for by the captain to receive his orders, when he was found to be drunk. When shall this besetting sin of our sailors be banished from their ocean homes? It is their curse. It was supposed that rough, bullying men made the best, and therefore were chosen for the office, of course with the other qualifications of good seamen; but as it rule they could do their share of "splicing the main brace," as drinking grog was called. But it is much altered since those days; the quantity of rum has been reduced, and tea and cocoa served instead, and many of the merchant service sail with no spirits.

Drunkenness

"Drunkenness nowadays in the Navy kills more men than the sword – I am sure of it."

Surgeon William Warner - 17 April 1813

Source: http://www.nationalarchives.gov.uk/surgeonsatsea/. This was a recent project to analyse the journals and diaries of Royal Navy surgeons between 1793 and 1880.

Tea and cocoa

Tea was introduced by the Royal Navy for issue to sailors in 1790. This was after the issue of sugar, coffee and hot chocolate commenced in 1780. These were actually introduced first in warm climates. Later a surgeon named Trotter suggested warm cocoa or hot chocolate would be good to help men warm up after a cold watch in the North Sea.

This was in addition to the gallon of beer each man received each day. Add rum and sometimes wine and it is no surprise there was a problem with drunkenness.

Now came the American War, and the causes of which were the celebrated "Orders in Council."

In 1806, after the defeat of the Prussians at Jena, Napoleon entered Berlin, and issued his celebrated "Berlin Decrees," by which he ordered the seizure of English property wherever it might be found, thus offering to other nations the opportunity of taking our merchandise, or ships in their ports, thereby seeking to ruin our trade. "The Orders in Council" were intended as a reprisal, and confiscated French property wherever it might be found, the French mercantile navy being almost destroyed. The Americans consequently carried on most of the commerce from neutral ports, therefore the enforcement of these orders was most annoying to them. If they carried French goods they would enter them in the ship's bill of lading, which was supposed to be it description of the ship's cargo, then she was likely to be taken because she was carrying French goods. Then if they carried them without entering in the bill, our cruisers, if they found them on board, seized the ship, although it was that of a neutral, the Prize Courts condemned her, and she became a lawful capture. These, and other grievances, led to the will- of 1813 and 1814. V1'e had six American merchant ships stopped by us, to see if they were carrying any French goods. As an instance we chased one ship and brought her to by firing at her, and sent a boat's crew to search her, but could find nothing. As they were going away, the officer in charge of the searching party heard one of the crew say that he would sell her for a glass of grog. On his return he reported this to the captain, who had her boarded again, and a more rigorous search made, when they found some cases of French watches that were not put down in the bill, seized her, and the court condemned her as a lawful prize.

We formed part of the squadron that ran up the Chesapeake, and diverted the attention of the American troops by running up the different rivers and destroying manufactories of war like material, alarming the whole country; then, as soon as the American troops began to march towards the threatened parts, we sailed clown again and up other rivers on the other side of the bay, keeping their troops marching and counter-marching, whilst our troops landed and defeated the American forces, although with the loss of General Ross; took Baltimore, marched on to Washington, burnt the public buildings, and re-embarked our troops. Soon after, Napoleon having abdicated, the power of France was shattered, the causes of the issue of the "Orders in Council" were removed, and negotiations for the ending of the war were brought to a successful issue. While we were up the Chesapeake, parties were continually being landed, at one place to destroy an iron-foundry where cannon were cast, at others to get supplies from the farmers, who, however, mostly left their farms and houses until the return of our parties to their boats.

Our supply of poultry was unlimited. They were brought away dead, but sometimes alive, and kept until they were wanted. The carpenter had bought some geese off some of the foraging parties, and was keeping them at the head of the ship, a place where they were out of sight. Captain Rechell took the captain of another ship of our squadron over the San Domingo to show him the old Spanish ship. When he came to the head he saw the geese, and being very orderly in these matters, inquired of the sailors whose they were? They replied the carpenter's. "Throw them overboard," he said. So the geese were soon floating on the surface of the sea quite enjoying a swim, and the carpenter was watching as the ship left them behind. Presently he saw a boat lowered from the ship following in our wake, and his geese captured and carried on board.

Our squadron was ordered home, so we bid farewell to the friends we had made during our stay at Halifax and elsewhere. For me it was like leaving home, having been ten years on the station. When we arrived in sight of the "White cliffs" of Old England orders were received for us to rendezvous at Spithead, to form part of the great fleet assembled to honour the presence of the allied sovereigns, Emperors of Russia and Austria, King of Prussia, and numerous princes, marshals, generals, etc., together with our Prince Regent and a brilliant staff. After their inspection of the fleet and blazing a few tons of gunpowder in saluting them, they returned to London, and the fleet dispersed.

We were ordered to Sheerness to be paid off, and on August 24th, 1814, ended my active foreign service; but I remained gunner of the San Domingo still, she being laid up in ordinary, so as to be ready for active service if required. On January 1st, 1817, I was appointed to the Redoubtable, and February 1st, 1824, to the Pitt, 74, at Portsmouth, and on November 3rd, 1828, to the Princess Charlotte, 120, and October 14th, 1831, to the Victory, 100, Nelson's old flagship, to be borne on her books, but lent to the Royal Naval College, Portsmouth, as Instructor in seamanship, rigging, and gunnery, the most important post for one of my rank to hold in the service. The period that the students remained was two years. We had a rigging house built with the roof high in centre for the masts and topmasts. On the floor, which represented the deck of a frigate and a brig, which only had two masts, there was a gunwale on the floor representing the sides of the ship, so as to have dead eyes and chains or channels to fasten the rigging outside. They had to rig each, begin with bare poles and put up every rope, make every knot, and there were some difficult ones to make, and splicing. By so doing they learned the name, use, and place of every rope in a ship.

At the corner of the north wall of the dockyard we had a two-gun battery of 9-pounders fitted like the side of a ship, where they went to drill and fire at three targets six hundred and ten yards distant.

They were allowed two shots, and if they struck the target received a shilling and another shot. One day one of the students hit it three times following. The Excellent gunnery ship lay close off our battery. Our senior lieutenant, a veteran with a wooden leg in place of one he lost in the passage of the Dardanelles under Admiral Duckworth, was chaffing the lieutenants of the Excellent that they were such a lot of duffers that he could beat them at any time with his boys. "Ah," said the other, "I saw your gunner pointing the gun for them."

"No you did not. I am always present, having charge of the firing party. They always go through the exercise under the gunner, and when ready to fire ask his opinion, and they act accordingly, and it is his place to instruct them."

Admiral Duckworth

Was a very able, though not outstanding, cautious leader. For these reasons he is not a particularly famous admiral in the history of the Royal Navy.

There are three notable facts about him, one bizarre, one ironic and one coincidental, which underlines why even those events that could have created fame for him do not really make the grade.

The bizarre is the story of how he received a concussion. This was while he was a lieutenant on HMS Princess Royal. He was hit on his head by the flying head of a sailor decapitated by a canon ball.

The ironic centres around his tendency to caution. Controlling a fleet of 12 ships he arrived at the island of Tenedos (Turkey) with orders to take possession of the Ottoman fleet at Constantinople. Despite knowing of a Turkish build up, meaning success would be most likely achieved with quick, decisive action, he waited in the strait. Subsequently one of his subordinates, Vice-Admiral Sir Sydney Smith, achieved an effective victory against the Turkish fleet, one therefore which could not be attributed to Duckworth.

The next day Duckworth's squadron carried out a diplomatic mission to take the British Ambassador Arbuthnot to meet the Sultan. This achieved nothing, this time not because of any fault in Duckworth but because he obeyed secret orders requiring caution.

On reaching Constantinople, Duckworth decided caution was the order of the day due to the substantial number of shore-based guns the Turks had available. He observed just how defensible the area was against any form of attack. Even though he retreated without risking any offensive action, his ships sustained damage and casualties as they withdrew.

The irony here is that history was to prove his caution on this occasion wholly correct. When British and French ships attacked in an attempt to take Constantinople just over 100 years later during the first world war, a large proportion of the battleships were sunk by mines laid by the Turks. This plan was sponsored by Winston Churchill.

Later, Anzac (Australian and New Zeeland) forces were landed. They suffered terrible losses due to being landed on open beaches against totally fanatical Turkish troops who always fought to the death. Eventually the Anzac forces had to be evacuated.

If Winston Churchill had known of, or taken note of Admiral Duckworth's assessment, history might not have recorded perhaps the most disastrous operation he sponsored during his otherwise mainly highly successful career.

Duckworth's coincidental claim to fame was that whilst the commander of the Plymouth Naval Base, following his capture and landing there, he was the last senior British officer to see and speak to Napoleon.

They also had two boats to sail about the harbour, and a cutter called the Dart, in which they sailed out to Spithead, or down the Solent.

I remained in the Naval College until it was abolished, May 25th, 1837, and was discharged the service on a pension of eighty-five pounds a year, the highest allowed, my whole service being forty-seven years, one month, three weeks, and three days, spent in Europe, Asia, Africa, and America, which is divided into ten years, three weeks, and three clays from my entrance as a boy until made warrant officer. Then seventeen years, eight months, three weeks and a day in active commissioned service, and seventeen years, eleven months, and three days of ordinary or harbour service.

At my discharge I was sixty-two years and nearly six months of age, quite serviceable, having been healthy all my life, thank the Lord.

Thus ends the log, full of interest to me, because it brings back to my memory the tales, yarns, and ghost stories that I listened to on winter nights around the galley fire, or summer's eve around the rudder head in the wardroom. I remember his orderly habits, and punctuality to duty, and his love of truth, so that his word was to be depended upon. Sir John S. Pechell, who was his captain twice in the Cleopatra and in the San Domingo, knew him, and was one of the Lords of the Admiralty that got him the appointment at the Royal Naval College, and knew he was qualified. Subjoined is a copy of his letter: -

Admiralty, August 25th, 1831,

"Mr. S -

"I understand that the situation of Gunner to the Royal Naval College is vacant, by the superannuation of Mr. Holman. You, of course, know what is required of persons to fill that situation. If you think it would be advantageous for you, I will endeavour to get it for you.

Yours,

"SAMUEL JOHN BROOKE PECHELL."

Even after the abolition he got. him an easy situation, which he could hold, and receive his pension. He resigned when he was nearly seventy, and lived to be eighty-two and six months, and was buried in Portsmouth cemetery.

The Government in 1848 made 'reparation for a long neglect in the granting medals, when he received one with four bars, and meeting an old admiral with whom he sailed when a midshipman, was asked by him how many bars he had, told* him four, and that of the actions with the Milan, in which they were taken, and the Guillaume Tell, which they captured, no notice was taken. He said "Write to the Admiralty, and state your case, and I will write also." He received two more bars. The third, the capture of the Topiaze, though off the Island of Guadaloupe, was included in the operations against Martinique.

He only wore it a few times, on anniversaries. On one occasion, whilst returning from a walk, he was stopped by some soldiers and hailed as "The Old Warrior ! "

PART II

Extracts of the best passages of Part II follow, finally the whole text for those who wish to read it.

Old Thomas Cranfield used to go, I think, to Kingsland to an early prayer meeting, where a good minister often gave a short address. One particular ruing he was longing for it word of exhortation, m the good man only told a little story, that some one had given him a very choice seed, and so anxious was he to sow it in the early morning, that resolved to do it immediately he awoke and dressed, before he even consulted the chart and prayer. He went into the garden and planted it. I was coining in when he heard the chirp of the bird, and turning round saw him fly from the spot ire he had planted the seed. He returned, and it evident the bird had been watching him plant and directly his back was turned, flew clown and stole it.

Thomas Cranfield

Thomas Cranfield was one of the first, if not the first person to open a free school for the poor in London, in Kingsland Road, Hackney. These were termed Ragged Schools for "ragged people." They provided the only chance from the late 18th century onward for poor people to obtain an education.

By the time of his death, Cranfield, a tailor, had opened 19 free schools.

Then running in a gale on the Goodwin Sands; the firing of the gun, showing the blue light, firing a rocket, the sea breaking right over her, the crew and passengers getting into the rigging, the approach of the lifeboat. Some quit their hold, and are drowned before the lifeboat nears the wreck. How many heart-rending scenes we are continually reading of, but worse is the" Shipwreck of Faith." All lost! No hope; gone forever! May God ever keep you; if in danger, get into the lifeboat. And if you lose everything you have you are safe.

Goodwin Sands

The Goodwin Sands is a 10-mile long sandbank off the coast of Deal, Kent, England. It is estimated 2000 ships have been wrecked there. Famous ones include ironically the South Goodwin Lightship.

Several naval battles have been fought nearby.

In 2011 a German Second World War Dornier 17 bomber was discovered there. It had crash-landed in 1940 having been shot down, then quickly had been covered by the sands. It was discovered after it became visible again. It has been recovered, is being restored, and is on display at RAF Cosford.

The sands may have been the location of the island of Lomea, which if it did exist was inundated probably before the Domesday Book was written in 1085-6.

In fact, England was joined to France until about 8000 years ago when the end of the last ice age created the English Channel that now separates Britain and continental Europe. The shallow area of the North Sea called Dogger Bank at the time formed the Dogger Hills.

Now comes the question, what is the wind? And we reply: Wind is air in motion, and to measure its speed or velocity, an instrument has been invented called an anemometer, which not only tells us its speed but its pressure. Seven miles an hour is called a "gentle air," fourteen miles" a light breeze," twenty-one "a good steady breeze," forty miles" a gale," sixty miles" a heavy storm," eighty to a hundred" a hurricane sweeping all before it."

Anemometer

Dr. John Thomas Romney Robinson of Armagh Observatory invented the first practical anemometer in 1846. It is simply a number of cups mounted on the top of a vertical spindle, free to rotate when blown round by the wind, hence measuring the wind speed and pressure. However, Leon Battista Alberti described an anemometer around 1450.

CHAPTER I

Now, here is the complete text of part 2.

"THERE GO THE SHIPS."

PSALM civ.

"THIS voyage" are words that were uttered by the great missionary traveller Paul - yes, and sailor too. How often we read of his taking ship. And "thrice was I shipwrecked;" and the account of "this voyage" is the most graphic ever written. Any sailor reading it will know that none but one accustomed to the sea could have done it. It was on the deck of a ship he was tossed and driven many days by the stormy wind on the Great or Mediterranean Sea, when he spoke of "this voyage."

We live on an island called" Great Britain," and there is the "silver streak" all around us. Boys and girls enjoy a trip to the seaside, and, looking across the ocean, and seeing the sails and smoke of the steamers, can say with David, "There go the ships," and in fine weather can enjoy a row or a sail. Ours is what is called "an insular position" in Europe.

We are islanders, and therefore more acquainted with the sea than other nations. Our boys will sail their boats on our ponds, or row on the rivers, or the ornamental waters in our parks.

One sings " The sea is England's glory," and the truth of this comes home to every heart in the British nation. The sea, all its surroundings and associations, are ever dear to Englishmen. Of the songs that are sung, the most popular are sea songs.

"The sea, the sea,

The blue, the fresh, the ever free!

Dibden stirred the very hearts of the people and others who followed in his strain. Who has not heard?

"Here a sheer hulk lies poor Tom Bowling

The darling of our crew,

No more he hears the tempest howling,

Since death has brought him too."

Or -

"There she lay, all the day.

In the Bay of Biscay, 0!"

and -

"Hearts of oak are our ships,

68

Jolly tars are our men."

No calamity stirs the national sympathy more deeply than a gallant rescue, like that achieved by Grace Darling and her father; or of noble self-sacrifice, as the loss of a lifeboat crew, or hairbreadth escapes at sea. "There go the ships." Let us consider them.

One writes: "In our school-boy days it was in making ships that we tested the metal of the first pocket-knife we had. And the music of the sea is the spell and inspiration under which a Briton passes restless from shore to shore. Through every valley of our isle, as through the hollows of the ocean, still the irresistible voice of the waves passes inland, and draws with the power of a magnet. or the voice of a siren the country lads, and woos them to the shore and these, gazing upon the boundless horizon, feel a desire to see what is beyond. "They that go down to the sea in ships, that do business in great waters. These see the works of the Lord, and His wonders in the deep."

I have often thought we are very much like ships. Often, when quite a lad, have I gazed on those enormous three-deckers, pierced for one hundred and twenty guns, that were building in our dockyards, on the slips from which they were to be launched, when I looked up standing under the stern, and saw twenty-six feet water mark, that was to be the draught when she was afloat, and then above that three gun decks, and the quarter-deck, and the poop rising above that again--altogether more than fifty feet deep and sixty feet wide, with a length of three hundred feet.. Then the immense amount of timber of such wonderful shapes and sizes, so nicely fitted as to make a complete structure, and strike the beholder with wonder. But they are a thing of the past, none building in our dockyards now.

David looked at his body and said "I am fearfully and wonderfully made, and that my soul knoweth right well." Our body is indeed," curiously wrought," wonderfully framed together, similar to ships in their construction; and so thought Dr. Watts when he wrote,

Strange that a harp of a thousand strings

Should keel in tune so long."

When a ship is launched upon the ocean it is for a voyage, and when we are launched forth on the ocean of life it is for a voyage. We will therefore learn some of the lessons taught.

I was born on the sea, on board the San Domingo, a Spanish 74-gun ship that was captured at Nelson's last grand victory at Trafalgar, where his last memorable signal was hoisted, "England expects every man to do his duty." And they did it, as you have read in this book. Not only in Trafalgar, but in every quarter of the world. The first eight years of my life were spent on board a man-of-war. I did not know so much about houses as ships, or rooms as cabins, or windows as ports. The deck was my playground. Here I trolled my hoop or spun my top.

When a ship is finished on the slip where she has been built, preparations are made for a launch, which is quite a festive occasion. The ship is decked with flags, as many as can get. on board do so, and then the ceremony of christening, or giving her a name, is performed by some lady breaking a bottle of wine on the head of the figure-head, and pronouncing her name, the best use they could make of the wine, far better than drinking it., for the figure-head has no brains to be affected by it.. The signal given, the men knock away what are called the dog-shores, and then she quietly glides down the slip, increasing her speed as she goes, and amidst hearty cheering, the waving of hats and handkerchiefs, she dashes into the ocean, that is to be her future home.

When we leave our homes to go forth into life it is our launch out into the ocean of life so unknown to us; it is mostly a joyful one, and full of expectations.

Returning once from a launch, when all around seemed so cheerful, an old sailor was resting his arm upon an anchor, with his hand to his head, and looking serious. One of our party went up to him, and said, "Why, Jack, are you looking so serious today?"

"Oh," said he, "I was just thinking what would be the future of that beautiful ship. I have known some that on their first voyage have come in collision with others, and sunk, or obliged to return their cargo and go into clock for repairs, whilst others have been on the coasting trade for nearly a century."

A short time since a ship was launched in the north, either Liverpool or Glasgow, and named the Duphne, capsized at the launch, and a number were drowned. It was thought best to change her name to Ianthe, and she was not far down the Irish Channel when she came in collision with another ship, and was obliged to return, unload, and repair. Her name was now changed to Rosebud. A capital flower is the rose, and the bud is full of promise, the flower of the future; so she was called the Rosebud, and went to sea, and got on shore going to Belfast, and was obliged to return for repairs after her cargo was taken out. How many rosebuds like her are blighted! Her career was nothing but disaster.

We did not wonder at the shadow of the dark cloud that flitted across the face of the old sailor. It is the future of the young that makes us sometimes feel sad, even when all around us seems so bright, and cheerful.

An artist called one day upon a friend, and was much struck with the beautiful innocent face of his curly-headed, rosy-cheeked little boy who was being lovingly fondled by his mother.

On reaching home he went to his studio, and put his impressions of the scene upon canvas, finishing it at his leisure. It was called "Innocence," and he would not part with it. Many years passed away, when a friend called upon him and asked him to go with him to the prison, to see a man under sentence of death, who was suffering an agony of remorse, having in a drunken fit killed his young wife. It was heart-rending to see his agony from remorse. It so impressed him, that he also put it on canvas, and when finished called them" Innocence" and" Guilt," making them companion pictures; and soon after the found they were pictures of one and the same. The innocent child had grown and bloomed into it drunken murderer. Alas, what a change. What an awful shipwreck of the future! Glorious institutions are our Bands of I-lope, to save our youths and maidens from the dreadful perils of the drinking customs of the country, that their future may be brighter. On this voyage steer clear of the intoxicating cup.

After the launch and the masts are in with the rigging complete, we get the stores on board, and let us be sure they are all good and serviceable. Remember they are for service, not for show; not shams or counterfeits, but the very best. No cheap inferior anchors. Let them be good, but especially the Anchor of Hope. Be sure you have that. Whatever storms, temptations, yea, hurricanes beset you, and endanger the precious cargo you carry on this voyage, all 'is safe, for the Anchor is" sure and steadfast." The sailors call the best anchor the, "sheet anchor;" that is the one they depend upon at the last extremity. Anchor of Hope. Glorious title; bright hope. And the boats must not be forgotten, with all the apparatus to lower them safely, and especially the lifeboats; these are the safest, f r if a sea fills them they soon right. Some one asked a French captain in a storm if he knew where he was." Oh yes," said he, "near the English coast, because of the lifeboats."

And then we must have our colours to hoist, and show what we are, and what we sail under. No false colours. It is pirates that hoist these. Theirs is not a white, but a black flag. They hoist false colours to deceive. Most have seen the picture of the pirate ship exhibiting false colours, and some of the crew playing instruments to deceive, whilst others are laying down on the deck out of sight with pistols and rifles. No false colours.

When Paul saw the sailors getting into a boat "under colour," as if they would take the anchors out, pretending this was what they were about to do --but they intended to have escaped to the shore, and left the prisoners and soldiers to their fate—as soon as this was found out, the soldiers cut the ropes, and the boat fell into the sea. Hoist the true colours, and, like Nelson at the Nile, nail them to the mast.

I have heard of some ship-owners who bought cheap life-belts, which were made of rag and paper instead of cork, and which, when used, would be soaked, and not support or save; instead of life-belts would be death to any one who used thin, not having buoyancy enough to keep a man up. And be sure you store your mind with good and useful information, - the history of your own country, the nations of antiquity, voyages, and travels, and every useful book. Spurn the trash that abounds, sensational novels and books of the Jack Sheppard type. Have the mind well stored with good sound knowledge, and thus you will gain what you can never lose.

I remember them putting six hundred tons of iron ballast on board the Pitt, 74, to increase her depth in the water, because her stores and guns were not on board; and if a captain of a merchant ship cannot get it cargo to come home he ballasts his ship by taking in shingle from the beach, or he is in danger of capsizing; Zeal might spread the sails to make a quick voyage, but if no knowledge for ballast, dangerous will be the issue.

And among the stores we do not want intoxicating drinks. I-lave no spirits on board. It was the letting fall of a lighted candle near a leaking spirit cask that set on fire the Kent East Indiaman in the Bay of Biscay, when so many lost their lives. And officers in command of ships that have been wrecked have stove the spirit casks, and let the contents run into the sea, to prevent the men rushing to it, and becoming so as not to be under control.

The idea of not being able to endure hardships without spirits or grog is almost too ridiculous to mention. Englishmen can endure any climate in the world, as we have nearly every one on the globe in our island home. The spirit casks should be forbidden stores.

As soon as the crew are on board the watch must be set. There is the first watch, from eight till twelve at night; the middle watch, from twelve till four; and the morning watch, from four till six; and after that the dogwatch.

Once I asked my father to let me keep watch with him it was the first watch, from eight to twelve. It was on board the Pitt, a 74-gun ship, in Portsmouth harbour. A lantern, with born sides, containing a tallow candle, with a red cotton wick, to show it belonged to the naval stores, was hung between the entering port, or ship's door and the bell, and a half-hour glass stood on a table under the lantern. At eight o'clock all the lights but this lantern were put out, and the bell struck eight, the half-hour glass turned over for the sand to run through, and when it was all through I turned it over again, and ran to the bell, struck one, and cried, "All's well." I should say the bell only strikes as high as eight, so that four o'clock, eight o'clock, and twelve o'clock, are eight bells, and half-past these hours, one bell. The other ships in the fleet followed, and there was quite a chorus of "All's well." But to see the watch is faithfully kept on board, a guard boat goes round the harbour, sometimes with muffled oars, to row without noise. And sometimes the officer in command had on canvas shoes, so that he could come up the ladder quietly, and see the watch was all right, if not, report him to the admiral. Should any boat pass the ship, the duty of the officer on watch would be to hail her, "Boat ahoy!" If nothing to do with the ships of the fleet, the answer would be, "Shore boat." If the guard boat, the answer by the officer in command would be" Guard boat."

A mast stood above the water at Spithead for some time. It was the mast of the Royal George, one hundred and twenty guns, which sunk there in a peculiar manner, August 29th, 1782. Two lighters were alongside, laden with provisions and stores, and the crew were mostly below stowing them away. They had heeled the ship to do some repairs below the water-line on one side, therefore had drawn the guns in and run them nearly to the centre of the ship. Thus, being heavier weighted one side than the other, brought that side when the guns were run in higher out of the water, and so the repairs were proceeding. Soon after the wind freshened, and the sea, washing against the portholes on the lower deck, was nearly washing in on the low side. The boatswain told the lieutenant, the officer of the watch, that he thought the position of the ship was dangerous, but he took no notice. At length, when spoken to again, he saw the danger, and all hands were piped to quarters, to pull the guns in their places, to right the ship. They pulled them up, but it was too late. She heeled right over, and all struggled to the portholes to get through, but scarcely any got out, for they were jammed in; and one who jumped from the deck into the sea described the sight as awful indeed, despair being depicted in every face. She sunk with nearly all her crew between decks, and nearly nine hundred persons, crew and visitors come to bid farewell, lost their lives, together with Admiral Kempenfeldt and nearly all the officers. I have often passed the large grave in Kingston churchyard where the bodies found were buried; most of them never came out of the ship, but were imprisoned there. "Here was a very careless watch." I have a box turned out of one of her timbers, blown up by Colonel Chesney in 1857 or thereabouts, so as to clear away the danger, and remove the buoy that marked the spot where her wreck lay. A gaze at this box, which I have had for fifty years, carries me back to its whole history. It was more than fifty years under water, and the ship was many years building, and it grew either in an English or Italian forest, and three or four hundred years before this some hog may have trodden an acorn into the earth from whence came this tree. I have only to look at my box, and in it is the whole story of the loss of the Royal George and the careless watch.

And there are times when we feel so secure and safe as not to watch at all. This feeling of self-security is very dangerous. The Master says," But I say unto you, Watch." One of our cruisers chased a French privateer schooner, but she escaped by running for Lisbon, and anchoring within fifty yards of Belem Castle, then in possession of the French. The captain of the cruiser withdrew to lull suspicion, but at dusk he ran in within three miles, and called for volunteers to man and arm a boat, to attempt to bring her out. When quite dark the boat started, and with muffled oars pulled close to her. So still was everything that they could hear the tread of the French sentinel on Belem Castle. Quietly they got alongside, and noiselessly boarded her, found no watch on deck, immediately put the hatches down quietly to keep the crew below, cut the cable, and shook out the topsail, and she quietly left the anchorage, the sentinel supposing it was her own crew that was running her out. In little more than an hour after being boarded she was anchored close to the cruiser, a prize, and her crew prisoners. There was no watch. Remember the Master's warning, "But I say unto you, Watch." They doubtless thought they were perfectly secure, and no one would dare approach near Belem Castle, with its heavy guns. Their security was false. Just what they supposed could not happen, did.

"Gird thy heavenly armour on,

Wear it ever night and day;

Near thee lurks the evil one;

'Watch and pray.'

"Hear the victors who o'ercame,

Still they mark each warrior's way;

All with warning voice exclaim,

'Watch and pray.'

"Hear above all, hear thy Lord,

Him thou lovest to obey;

Hide within thy heart His word,

'Watch and pray.'

"Watch, as if on that alone

Hung the issue of the day;

Pray that help may be sent down:

'Watch and pray.'

CHAPTER II

This Voyage

We have seen the importance of setting the watch; the next thing is to get the compasses adjusted and rightly fixed, and thus prepare for," this voyage." What a curious thing is the magnetised needle, nicely balanced, and always true, pointing to the north. The ship is to be steered, guided by this.

Conscience is your compass. Keep it true, ever steer by it, listen to its voice, let it speak, never stifle it. The first wrong thing you do it will speak. A boy has got upon a chair during the absence of his mother to reach the jam pot in the cupboard; he hears the handle of the door rattle. How sharp he gets down; how the colour comes into his face. He looks quite confused. Why? That is conscience speaking. The other day I took hold of a piece of black hot iron, thinking it was cold, but it burnt my thumb and finger; the skin was quite dead, and I could not feel. If you do not listen to conscience it will not speak so loud next time; and if you continue to refuse to hear it, its voice will be gradually hushed, and by-and-by not speak at all. Don't let your conscience be stifled, scared, but ever listen to its voice.

At t he Nile expedition, the box where the compass was fixed in the boats was painted with white phosphoric paint, which took in the light during the day, and gave it out at night, so the position of the needle could always be seen, and the boats steered aright. Let the light of God's Word ever shine on your conscience, your compass, and you will not mistake the way it points. Follow it.

When about seven years of age I sailed from Sheerness to Portsmouth, and somewhere off the Sussex coast the master and the mate at night had different opinions about a light shown by a light ship moored on a sand. It was thought safest to anchor for the night. Being in bed, in a bunk as it is called, a sort of a big cupboard into which you crawl through a hole, and when inside there is plenty of room to lay down, and no fear of falling out. I remember as vividly as if it was only yesterday the gentle ripple of the water against the side of the vessel close to my ear. They were talking very quietly, so I sat up and peeped at them. They had the table spread over with charts, and were looking for the lightships and sands, -- for these are all marked down in the charts, -- the depth of the water, what kind of bottom, and all the information necessary. Don't forget the chart! The Bible is the chart, where all the rocks and sands are marked down; all the line of the coast is shown; where the lighthouses are; what. kind of lights they show; where the lightships are moored how deep the water is; what kind of bottom. All these are important; all in the Bible. Very important to know the depth.

A 74-gun ship was at anchor in Table Bay when a storm arose, and the water not being very deep she plunged between the seas and struck the fluke of her own anchor. Owing to the shortness of her cable and the shallowness of the water she became a wreck. It is necessary to know the depth and the bottom that the anchors do not drag.

See a gallant ship that left the port, fairly and bravely rigged, with all her colours flying, cleaving her way through the high sea, which is as unwrinkled as the brow of childhood, and seems to laugh with many a twinkling smile; and when night falls, the moonbeams play on many a wave, and the brightness of the day has left a delicious balminess behind it in the air, and the ship is anchored in a treacherous bottom, and soon all in her is still, save the gentle drowsy gurgling that tells that water is the element in which she floats; hut. in the (lead of the night the anchor loses its hold, mid then the current., deep and powerful, bears her noiselessly whither it will, and in the morning the wail of desperation rises from her, for she has fallen on a shoal, and as the breeze springs up with the daylight, rudely dashes her planks against the shoal, contrasts strangely with the peacefulness of the past evening. How important good anchorage ground.

Be sure you do not forget the chart; consult it every day. If you do not belong to the International Bible Reading Association, join at once, so to study it every day. The directions are so in, "That the wayfaring man, though a fool, shall err therein." Don't forget the chart.

Old Thomas Cranfield used to go, I think, to Kingsland to an early prayer meeting, where a good minister often gave a short address. One particular ruing he was longing for it word of exhortation, m the good man only told a little story, that some one had given him a very choice seed, and so anxious was he to sow it in the early morning, that resolved to do it immediately he awoke and dressed, before he even consulted the chart and prayer. He went into the garden and planted it. I was coining in when he heard the chirp of the bird, and turning round saw him fly from the spot ire he had planted the seed. He returned, and it evident the bird had been watching him plant and directly his back was turned, flew clown and stole it.

It taught him a lesson he never forgot. Consult chart the first thing every morning.

An affecting story is told of an American gentleman who gave the first steam-printing machine to the American Sunday School Union. He sat down to breakfast one morning, and was scanning over the morning paper, when his little son got on his knee, gently pulled the paper out of his hand, saying,

Ii a smile," Papa, Bible first; papa, Bible first." Yes, the chart first. This lesson was never forgotten; always after the "Bible first." His son soon after was taken ill, and died, and the printing machine was a token of remembrance of the lesson taught.

We want next a pilot, one who knows all about the rocks, sandbanks, and currents in the part where they are. A drunken pilot, who had been dismissed, once brought an American frigate, in 1816, with the ambassador on board, into Spithead. How dangerous to be in the hands of drunken pilots.

An American frigate was running for New York, pursued by three British men-of-war closing around her, and escape seemed impossible without running through the passage known even now as "Hell Gate." The rocks here are dreadful and dangerous. Only a year or two since the American government., at an enormous expense, blew up great reefs of these rocks, and many years before blew up a number of others; but at this time none had been removed. The British ships forced upon her, and one ball cut the American captain off the taffrail into the sea. Some of the officers wanted a boat lowered to pick him up.

No," said the pilot, he has died a warrior's death. To lower a boat in this sea would be to lose more lives. We must run through Hell Gate, as the only way of escape." The sea was dashing furiously on the rocks, one sheet of nothing hut white foam before them. He turned her course into Hell Gate, and steered her safely through the boiling sea. The danger was awful in the extreme.

When he resolved to run through it was blowing it furious gale. He stood over the compass and "conned" the ship; that is, gave directions how to steer to the man at the wheel; and close to the rocks he went, with the breakers furiously dashing over them. Not one word did he speak, except in directing, until she was safe through. The British men-of-war were afraid to follow.

The Great Pilot is the Lord Jesus Christ.

With Christ in the vessel I smile at the storm."

He is the Pilot to have on board. He will run you safely by the Rock of Hell Gate. "They shall not prevail against you." Do not go on such a voyage without such a Pilot. He knows the coast, and all its dangers. Come to Him as the disciples did in the storm on the Lake of Galilee. They cried, "Lord, save, or we perish." He rose from his pillow, and hushed the storm in an instant with, "Peace, be still;" and as they neared the shore all was calm and still.

Christ's first disciples were sailors; and the scene on the lake is beautifully described by Bishop Heber: -

"When through the torn mil the wild tempest is streaming,

When o'er the dark waves the red lightning is gleaming,

Nor hope lends a ray the poor seamen to cherish,

We fly to our Saviour--' Save, Lord, or we perish.'

"Jesus, once rocket gut the breast of the billow,

Aroused by the shriek of despair hum Thy pillow,

Now seated in Glory, the mariner cherish,

Who cries in his anguish, 'Lord, save, or we perish.'"

As we are now

"Out on the ocean Sailing,"

Therefore we must look out, for "squalls."

A squall is a sudden gust of wind that comes with little or no warning. Lakes, surrounded by mountains and valleys, are frequently visited with squalls, as the wind rushing down the ravines and valleys comes suddenly. Therefore, a good lookout must be kept. They are very dangerous. I heard my father say, that just before a white squall which they had prepared for, a beautiful schooner was seen in full sail, and after it was over she was nowhere to be seen, had gone clown, with every sail set. She had not prepared for it.

I was in a white squall at Spithead in a sailing-boat, the wind contrary, or, as the sailors say, "right in our teeth." We had to get on board an East Indiaman to do some work required to a carriage, therefore had to heat out against the wind, that is, to sail in a zigzag way; and we had just, reached Fort Monckton, to make the final tack to the ship. The sun was shining brightly, when suddenly a white mist obscured Hyde, and the boatman said to us, "Prepare, gentlemen, for it's coming." We secured ourselves in the boat, -- and it did come, rain and blow, nothing to he seen but Spithead, one vast sheet of foam, and the rout terrible indeed. The boy attending to the foresheets was hid by the spray flying over, and the man stood with the other sheets in his hand and the rain streaming off his nose, ready to let go the sheets in a moment of danger. It was an awful ten minutes. When the sun burst out again we were nearly alongside the Indiaman.

So in life's voyage, sudden temptations are like white squalls. They come fiercely, and threaten with instant, destruction; but we must ever be on the watch, and ever prepared to meet them.

Then there are the gales, not like the squalls, short, fierce, and soon over. A gale sometimes continues a long time; not only a day, but many days. The gale Paul was in continued many days; and so wearying and exhausting that the sailors gave up in despair, losing all hope. So it may happen to us, as to the good men of old; trouble and difficulties coming one after the other upon its so quickly, until there seems no end of them, and, like the Psalmist, they ask, "Will the Lord cast off forever? Will He be favourable no more? Is His mercy clean gone forever? Doth his promise fail for evermore? Hath God forgotten to be gracious? Hath He, in His anger, shut up His tender mercies?" But when He thought of the hell gates he had weathered, and saw the bright pole-star shining through the gloomy sky, he felt it was wrong to despair, although the gale had been long and fierce, and looking up with brighter eyes he exclaimed, "This is my infirmity, but I remember the years of the Most High!" For by His help he had come through all safely.

There are other dangers besides gales, sometimes want of wind. My father once sailed across the Straits of Gibraltar to the African coast to see if any French ships were attempting to raw through under cover of the night. They sailed over until near the African coast, and put the ship about to run back, but the wind fell, and the high land prevented what little was left from filling the topsails, and the ship drifted stern foremost towards the rocky coast. He was sent down to the captain by the officer of the watch to let him know of the critical state of the ship. "Is the master on deck?" was the reply. "If so, I can do nothing more." The master was looking silently over the stern into the darkness, and listening to the awful sound of the breakers on the rocks. It was a beautiful moonlight night, but the high land hid the moon, and all was dark. The sailors were busy aloft bracing top and topgallant sails, first to the starboard, then to the larboard side to catch the little puffs of wind that came over the high land on the right and then the left. These light and variable breezes are called by the sailors "cat's paws," from being like the short stroke of it cat's paw when playing.

Still the ship was going backward to all appearance to destruction, when it stronger "cat's paw" came over the high land, filled the sails that had been braced round to receive it, and took her out into the Straits.

Here, as often elsewhere, "Man's extremity is God's opportunity." Look well after the opportunities, the "cat's paws." The loss of them has been the ruin of millions. Watch for them. Napoleon was once riding down in the front of his troops unattended, when his horse ran away with him. A soldier dashed

out of the ranks, and at the risk of his life stopped the horse and saved the Emperor, who said to the soldier, "Thank you, captain." Now was his opportunity, and he said, "Sir, what regiment?"

"The Guards," was the reply. The soldier immediately posted off to where the Guards were drawn up, and

reported his promotion by the Emperor to a captaincy in the Guards. He watched for the opportunity.

There is a grand one now, for "Now is the accepted time, now is the day of salvation." "Today, if ye will hear His voice, harden not your hearts." Now is the opportunity; embrace it.

There are undercurrents. The wind may blow one way and the current run another, and endanger the course of the ship, therefore they like to take an observation of the sun, and see where they are, for the undercurrent may take them out of their course, and lead them to some rock or sandbank they wished to avoid, and therefore they must alter their course.

There are undercurrents that will take us right out of our course--the insinuations of friends and relations, the influence of some companions, the continued chaff, the sneering ridicule. It is distressing to read of the wreck of some ship which lost her reckoning, and struck on a rock they knew nothing about. Had the reckoning been made up every day they would have seen where they were, but the undercurrent would alter all that, and therefore must be reckoned. In some parts they know the force of a current that crosses their course; they call it "leeway." They have to allow for it, and steer accordingly. Beware of the undercurrents. They are so quiet. Take your latitude and longitude; consult your chart, the grand old chart.

The River Mississippi near its mouth is very deep, the channel is worn so by the continual running of the immense volume of water. The wind sometimes is directly opposite to the current, and drives the water back on the surface, but the undercurrent beneath the surface and the wind's power flows on.

Be not deceived with the appearance of the surface.

I was trolling my hoop round the deck of the Princess Charlotte, a 120-gun ship in Portsmouth Harbour, when the sound of some one singing arrested my attention, and running to the entering port, I saw the Tyne frigate sailing into the harbour under topsails, and it man in the chains heaving the lead. That instant he threw it into the sea, and cried out in a musical tone, "By the deep nine;" that is, nine fathoms (fifty-four feet) of water. Hauling up the lead he threw it again, and cried out, "Quarter less seven;" that was twelve feet six inches less water. The order was immediately given, "Let go the anchor," stopping the ship and furling the sails. Had they proceeded any further they would have risked running aground.

It is very interesting in reading of Paul's shipwreck of sounding, casting out the anchors, and "wishing for day." Essential to know how we are sailing. Many a fine ship has been lost through neglecting to take the soundings, and many a man has been ruined through neglecting this important duty, and thinking he was all right, has run ashore when he least expected it; and so in the heavenly voyage" continual soundings" are necessary to know "All's well."

What a terrible thing is a shipwreck! And how numerous the causes-- awful collisions at night, when ships at anchor have been cut down, and hundreds gone to the bottom in their beds. The cutting down of the Princess Alice on the Thames. Collisions in the day, striking on the rocks and holes made in the bottom, the water rushing in, the frantic screams of frightened men and women, the rush to boats, the swamping and drowning of the whole.

Then running in a gale on the Goodwin Sands; the firing of the gun, showing the blue light, firing a rocket, the sea breaking right over her, the crew and passengers getting into the rigging, the approach of the lifeboat. Some quit their hold, and are drowned before the lifeboat nears the wreck. How many heart-rending scenes we are continually reading of, but worse is the" Shipwreck of Faith." All lost! No hope; gone forever!

May God ever keep you; if in danger, get into the lifeboat. And if you lose everything you have you are safe.

There was a picture exhibited in the Royal Academy a few years since, "The White Cliffs of Old England." It represented a porthole in the side of a ship, and a group of sailors, with smiling faces, looking through and seeing the white cliffs of the southern coast, engaged in deep and earnest conversation. One of the older ones was doubtless talking about his wife, wondering how he should find her, and how his girls and boys had grown, -- should he know them? -- and what a glad welcome he should receive. Others of the younger ones were wondering how the "old folks" looked, and their brothers and sisters were. Others were thinking of their sweethearts and of the presents they had brought them from foreign parts; how glad they would be to receive them, and prize them; the stories they would have to tell them of what they had seen, and of the storms they had weathered. That is something of the thoughts the picture conveyed to me. But they were all expecting to meet in the Haven of Rest those they loved.

What enjoyment after being tossed on the billows of the stormy sea! The end of the voyage of life should be the Haven of Rest, not of idleness. It will be a rest from the storms and cares of life. No raging storms, no fierce squalls, no deceitful calms, no empty whistling winds, no darkness, no fogs, but all love, joy, light, and peace; when we shall go on increasing in knowledge; when we shall "know even as we are known;" when the great mysteries of Providence and Grace will be solved we understood not. Now we see through a glass darkly, but then it will be face to face, leaving the wonders of the past, and basking in the sunshine of His favour, to go out no more, but to enjoy a never-ending felicity in the presence of the Great King and His holy angels, and the spirits of the just made perfect.

But this happiness will only be ours if we have the compass pointing true, the chart ever before us, and the Great Pilot to guide us in our course.

Chapter III

WINTER and spring are the seasons for winds.

Wintry gales are often accompanied by blinding snowdrifts and sleet, frequently benumbing the hands and feet of our brave seamen.

Often on a wintry night have I been sitting round the galley fire on hoard a man-of-war, the wind roaring down the funnel, causing the sympathetic remark, "Oh, the poor souls at sea I."

In our island home we are more familiar with the wind and its effects on the ocean, which lashes our coasts; thus we are able to study the laws that govern the windy storms. Telegrams now come from the other side of the Atlantic, telling us of the probability of a storm reaching our coasts in such and such a quarter; and messages are sent by telegraph to the different seaports, to warn captains of ships about to sail of the approaching danger, and all around our coasts, on the most dangerous spots, are stationed lifeboats, that are manned by volunteers, who rush to the rescue in the time of danger, many of which have been presented by benevolent individuals to aid in saving the lives of our brave seamen. Two of these boats have been purchased by the pence of the Sunday scholars. We see what trifles can do, and I think it is time that another Sunday School lifeboat was being built.

Storms are sure to drive ships on some part of our coast. If they are westerly gales then the eastern coasts are free from danger, and if easterly winds then the western coasts are the safest; but the captains of most ships make for some port or safe anchorage to ride out the storm, and if they part with their anchor they hoist a signal of distress, and the nearest lifeboat station, on receiving the signal, man their lifeboat and launch.

"Through the wild surf they cleave their way,

Lost in the foam, nor know dismay,

For they go the crew to save."

Now comes the question, what is the wind? And we reply: Wind is air in motion, and to measure its speed or velocity, an instrument has been invented called an anemometer, which not only tells us its speed but its pressure. Seven miles an hour is called a "gentle air," fourteen miles" a light breeze," twenty-one "a good steady breeze," forty miles" a gale," sixty miles" a heavy storm," eighty to a hundred" a hurricane sweeping all before it."

The pressure of wind the speed of which is five miles an hour is two ounces on a square foot, gradually increasing until the pressure is fifty pounds, or a hurricane speed of eighty to a hundred miles an hour. In the great storm that passed over London February 6th, 1867, the anemometer at Lloyd's registered thirty-five pounds to the square foot, and the wind during that storm acquired a speed of eighty-three miles an hour. The great storm that in 1703 swept away Eddystone lighthouse, and did immense damage all round our coasts, and particularly in London, led to it sermon being preached in Great Wild Street. Chapel, Lincoln's Inn Fields, from that time until now with very few exceptions, and called 'The Great Storm Sermon."

All wind is caused directly or indirectly by a change of temperature. Suppose the temperature of two adjoining regions to become different, one hotter and the other colder; the air of the warmer will become lighter and ascend, the cold air being heavier, will flow in to take its place. Stand upon a pair of steps, and ascend until your head is near the ceiling, and you will find it very warm, the gas or lamp making it so. Open the door of a warm room, and you feel the rush of the cold air. "That is wind."

There are "constant winds," and from the benefits they confer upon our merchants are called" trade winds." When a part of the earth's surface is a whole zone or division of the earth, as in the tropics, a surface wind will set in towards the heated tropical zone from both sides, and uniting, will ascend, and then separating, will flow as an upper current in opposite directions. Hence a surface current will flow from time higher latitudes towards the equator, and an upper current towards the poles. If then, the earth were at rest, and not moving at all, we should have a north wind in the northern half and a southern wind in the southern half of our globe. But this is modified or its form changed by the motion of our earth, which at the equator moves seventeen miles a minute towards the east, but at sixty degrees eight and a half, and at the poles nothing. Hence, the wind, arriving at places that move faster, "lags" behind; so the same wind becomes a contrary wind. This is very interesting, but we can only just look at it. When once the mariner can get into the "trade winds" he knows how far he can sail with the wind in one direction.

There is a region of calms at the equator, when the north and south trade winds unite and neutralise each other, but here heavy rains and thunderstorms prevail.

There are periodical winds, land and sea breezes. On the coast within the tropics a breeze sets in from the sea; at first a mere "breathing," but gradually increasing toward the middle of the day to a "stiff breeze," after which, toward evening, it falls to a calm. Soon after a contrary breeze springs up, and blows during the night towards the sea, and then dies away, to give place to the "sea breeze."

These winds are caused by the earth getting more heated than the sea, so the air over it ascends, and the cool air from the sea flows on to the land to supply its place, and during the night, the earth getting cooler than the sea, the air becomes heavier or denser, and flows out as it "land breeze."

The inhabitants of some regions, particularly the "Levant," call the breeze that comes from the sea sunrise "the doctor," from its cooling and refreshing influences in clearing away the infected air. What an illustration of Mal. iv. 2: "The Sun of Righteousness shall arise with healing in His wings." How like this refreshing breeze is Christ when He shines into any heart. His beams of light drive out the darkness, and shine into every crevice, cleansing and purifying. "He is the Doctor," yea, more; He is the "Great Physician of souls," who "cleanse from every impurity and renovate."

Has He shone into your heart? Have you felt s healing beams? As the morning flowers open receive the beams of the sun, so may your art, like Lydia's, open to receive "the light of the world."

There are "variable winds" caused by local circumstances, such as the figure of the country. Forests or tins, mountains or valleys, seas or lakes, surrounded high mountains, are dangerous, caused by the air rushing through the valleys. The lakes of Cumberland and Westmoreland in our own country, Killarney in Ireland, and the Lake of Galilee referred in the Gospel, are peculiarly subject to them. Hence the storm on the lake, and the dismay of disciples, although hardy seamen, exclaiming, "Lord, save, or we perish." Amid the howling storm the Lord of winds and waves rises from His pillow, and with the majesty and authority of King exclaims, "Peace, be still." And in an instant calm followed, the surface of the lake is ruffled, reflecting the stars and cities on its banks. We have the "simoon" or hot wind of the desert.

The sand getting heated by the sun to two hundred degrees, or nearly boiling water heat, the air resting on it becomes hot, and gives rise to ascending currents of air. Consequently cold air flows in on all sides towards these heated places, and these currents meeting, cause cyclones or whirling masses of air to be formed, which, swept forward by the wind, carry all before them.

It is this glowing heat of the wind, and its parching dryness, which is so destructive to human life. Its approach is indicated by it thin haze, which, becoming more dense, soon overspreads the whole sky.

Fierce gusts of wind follow, accompanied by clouds of red and burning sand, which look like vast columns of dust whirling round and forward, and huge mounds of sand are transferred from place to place by the terrible energy of the storm. They last from six to twelve hours.

Cambyses, a Persian king, marching to plunder the temple of Jupiter Ammon, situated in an oasis in the desert, perished, with fifty thousand of his soldiers, by the terrible simoon. It is also supposed that Sennacherib's army encamped round Jerusalem was destroyed by the hot wind suffocating them, Hezekiah being saved according to Isaiah's prophecy:

"Stormy wind fulfilling His word."

The Puna winds prevail for four months in the year, in it high barren tableland in Peru, called the "Puna." As they are a part of the east trade wind, after crossing the Andes Mountains, they are drained of their moisture, and consequently are the most dry and parching winds in the world. In travelling across the Puna it is necessary to protect the face with a mask from the heat and glare of the sun by day, and from the extreme cold by night.

The east winds that prevail here in the spring are part of the Great Polar current, which at that season descends over Europe, through Russia. This accounts for their dryness and unhealthiness. They are especially dreaded by the nervous and invalids, which has given rise to the well-known doggerel lines: --

"The wind is in the east,

Good for neither man nor beast."

Deaths from brain disease and consumption reach their highest during their prevalence in this country.

There are many influences that affect the winds, some purely local, -- the nature of the ground they pass over, whether clothed with trees or bare; their external form, whether level or mountainous; the vicinity of lakes or seas; and the passage of storms.

What a mighty force is wind, and all under God's direction. Let us think of the poor souls on the bosom of the stormy ocean. How often, when the storm has roared down the galley funnel on board the ship anchored in the harbour, words of pity for those exposed and the memories of past storms passed vividly before the minds' eyes of the "Old Salts" gathered round the fire. What a beautiful hymn is that of Bishop Heber! In his day they had to go round the Cape of Good Hope to get to India. And doubtless he experienced many a storm.

Winds have played an important part in the world's history. A wind assisted in drying the earth after the flood. A strong east wind blowing all night opened the passage of the Red Sea. A strong wind brought the flocks of quails around the camp, and supplied Israel with flesh, A wind smote the four corners of Job's sons' house they were feasting in, and buried them in the ruins.

Job and David speak of the wicked as "the chaff or stubble scattered by the wind." In the days of Elijah, after three years and six months without rain, according to his word, "The heavens were black with wind and clouds." Hosea says, "Ephraim feedeth upon the wind," that was in vain hopes of deliverance by Assyria; and in the Sermon on the Mount the closing passages contain," And the rains descended, the floods came, and the winds blew." And those who are wavering, not firm in their doctrine and Christian faith, are" Blown about by every wind of doctrine," not firm or certain. The Psalmist speaks of" Bringing the wind out of His treasuries," and as "gathering the wind in His fists." Xerxes, the Persian king, invaded Greece with the largest fleet and army that is recorded in history, and although he whipped the sea and put it in chains, he could not subdue it. His immense fleet was scattered, and he was compelled to cross the Hellespont in a little boat to get back to Asia.

The Spanish Armada sailed from Lisbon three hundred years ago, under their celebrated admiral the Marquis of Santa Cruz, and soon after were shattered by a storm, and obliged to return to repair their damages. Whilst refitting at Lisbon their admiral and the next in command died. They sailed again, and were attacked in the British Channel, and a number destroyed and taken. They were obliged to sail to the northward, and when off Flamborough Head it terrible storm scattered them, and seventeen of their ships were wrecked, and most of their crews lost.

Captain Wilson, who took out the first missionaries to the South Seas in the ship Duff to Tahiti, was a man opposed to religion, not believing in the existence of it God, the Bible, or Christian ministers. He endured great hardships in India, but was a man of an iron constitution and great bodily strength. He was taken prisoner by Hyder Ally, made his escape by jumping from a fort into the river, swam to the opposite bank; and so full of crocodiles was the river, that Hyder Ally would not believe he ever did it. He was finally captured and confined in a dungeon, being chained to another prisoner. Many a morning he had to be unchained, for his companion had died in the night, and he was chained to another. This happened several times, and doubtless Paul refers to this custom when he says, "Who shall deliver me from this body of sin and death?" At length he was released, and when he had recovered his strength took the command of a ship; but, in common with it number of other captains, he was windbound in a harbour which they could not get out of until the wind changed. One night he was on shore with the captains of the other ships drinking and gambling, when a quarrel took place. He put on his hat and returned to his ship. No sooner had he put his foot on the deck than the wind changed favourable to get out of the harbour. He instantly had the anchor weighed, the canvas unfurled to the breeze, and out she went. The news soon spread that Wilson was getting out. The other captains returned, but before they could start the wind came back to the old quarter, and they were all windbound.

He arrived at the port where his cargo was urgently required, and sold his entire cargo for almost whatever he liked to ask, making a fortune by this singular event--the change of the wind at that particular time. He resolved to retire. Returning to old England for that purpose, he settled down at Horndean, making his niece his housekeeper, who was a member of a Baptist church in Portsea, and driving her down on a Sunday to her chapel. Although bitterly opposed to Christianity, he had respect for other people's opinions, so he waited for her and brought her back. He had for a neighbour a captain of marines, a Christian man, with whom he often held arguments. This good man, feeling he was not able to argue with him, asked him to dine with him on a certain clay when he had invited his young minister to dine. That just pleased Captain Wilson. The day came, and they met to dine. After dinner Wilson was eager for the fray, and wished to begin; but the Rev. John Griffin suggested they should retire by themselves to an arbour in the garden, whilst the other guests walked over the grounds. The sun was near setting, painting up the sky, and all was peaceful and quiet. The discussion began and continued for some time, when he found he was in the hands of an abler man than he had ever met before, and that some of his opinions were very much shaken. On the next Sunday, when lie had driven his niece to her chapel, he thought he would just go round to Orange Street and hear this young man. They were singing the hymn before the sermon when Mr. Griffin saw him come in. He was preaching; a course of sermons on the eighth chapter of Romans, and knowing how infidels ridiculed those doctrines, wished he had any other subject to preach upon. "No," thought he, "I will preach it," and he did; and under God's blessing there came another influence "like a wind," that changed his whole life to one of devotion to that Saviour he had before rejected. Under a sermon by Mr. Griffin on Abraham leaving his home and friends, he was led to offer his services to the London Missionary Society, to take out the missionaries to Tahiti in the ship Duff, and to take a cargo suitable for disposal, so as to pay the expense of the voyage.

What a remarkable change of wind, to lead to such an issue. It was in the calm of the evening hours that Nicodemus came to Jesus to question Him upon the truths He had been preaching about, and Jesus spoke to him about the operation of the Holy Spirit as the "wind." We hear the sound thereof, but cannot tell whence it cometh nor whither it goeth. We see the effects of the wind, sometimes uprooting majestic oaks, levelling great buildings, piling the waters of the ocean in heaps, and engulfing the helpless mariner; or it comes as the cooling breeze in summer, or the gentle zephyr at eventide, greatly refreshing us after the heat of the day. We know not the exact laws that regulate the wind, but we see the effects. Thus it is with the work of the Holy Spirit. We see men and women, youths and maidens, whose hearts have been touched, changed, but we don't know how. The Holy Spirit, like wind, has blown as a Spirit of remembrance, and there has been a resurrection of the kind earnest, words of some teacher, or some address in the Sabbath School, some text or letter, or the death of a friend, and a change is seen -- a great change, a complete turning round. A new life, before sinful, now striving after holiness, loving what they hated before, and hating what they loved before; the thoughtless and frivolous are thoughtful, the prayerless are prayerful, the rebellious meek and gentle. Reader, is your heart renewed, your pride of heart humbled, your sin subdued, your soul comforted? If so, you possess a calm and a peace you cannot find words to express, but you know that joy and peace are yours. You may not be able to argue on the evidences of Christianity, but like the blind man you can say, "Whereas once I was blind, but now lean see." I know I possess joy and peace, and it has all been brought about by the mysterious operation of God's Holy Spirit. Various are the operations of the wind, so of the Spirit of God. David says in a Psalm, "He restoreth my soul." We often see in picture-dealers' windows

"Pictures restored;" and as an example a picture is exhibited, one half restored, cleaned, and looking lifelike, and the other half so grimy and foul looking, that we can scarcely make out what it is.

The restoration of our better nature is the work of the Spirit of God, Who comes like the wind, and cleanses and restores. Some, as Lydia, are subdued by the gentle influence like a zephyr, and the Sun of Righteousness shining into the opening heart expands it to receive its healing beams. With others nothing but the mighty, windy storm can break down and subdue their fierce opposition, and by sweeping away all their prejudices, produce a calm. It was so with the Philippian gaoler, -- one hour rudely thrusting them into the inner prison, and making their feet fast in the stocks, the next hour quickly releasing them, calling for mercy, washing their stripes, and setting refreshment, before them. What a change! Let us not, grieve the Holy Spirit of God.

"Holy Spirit, dwell with me

I Myself Would holy be;

Separate from sin, I would

Choose and cherish all things good,

And whatever I can be

Give to Him Who gave me 'Thee.'"

CHAPTER IV

The Measured Mile, or Trial Necessary

Little children, as soon as they can run about, catch hold of everything they see, and the mother carefully moves them out of the way, to prevent them hurting themselves or breaking the things. But there comes a time when they are grown a little bigger, that things are not moved out of their way, and mother, holding up her finger, says, "You must not touch." The child wonders, "Why not? I always did." The mother again says you must not touch," and this is a trial to the child. "Shall I touch and disobey my mother; or shall I obey?" But we don't know what we are until we are tried.

There is in the rifle factory al Birmingham what is called the "proof room." All the rifle barrels are tested here, "tried." They are loaded with heavy charge, of powder and fired, then allowed to stand some time; then they are all examined to see if they are sound, if not, they are thrown aside as useless, and the others are passed as proved.

At Spithead there is what is called the "Measured Mile." A buoy is moored at each end, and when the ship is ready for trial she is brought out to the spot with the steam up, having on board the builder, the engineer, and all others interested in the ship, with the representatives of the government for whom she has been built. She waits some time a distance from the mile, until all is ready. Then she starts so as to get tip the speed by the time she gets to the first buoy. Then the chronometers are noted as to the time, and revolutions of the engines counted, the hearings watched--are they cool or hot? Is the motion easy? When the end of the mile is reached, the time by the chronometers noted, the speed ascertained, the faults detected, and alterations suggested for her improvement, she is taken hack to the dockyard and the alterations completed, and tried again.

Now we can see the necessity of this trial, for it sometimes shows a flaw brought into sight by the strain. Perhaps the boiler is not strong enough. Had it not been for the trial it could not have been seen. It was the testing that brought it out.

Now suppose the ship had been sent, to sea with all her valuable stores on board, and the still more valuable lives of her crew and officers, numbering three or four hundred, and the steering gear or t he machinery failed in a gale in the Bay of Biscay, and all been lost, -- the ship sinking and the crew drowned. There would have been a general cry of indignation throughout the land on the folly of sending a ship to sea untried. Trial is quite necessary, for many things look well, but when tried found worthless. Many persons seem all right until we have dealings with them, and then, to our sorrow, we find out they are not what they appeared to be.

Trial is to bring out the good as well as the bad, that one may be preserved and the other cast aside as worthless. Great masses of quartz rock are brought under the crushing mills, that pound and crush it small. Now suppose the quartz could feel and speak, what would it say? Why are you pounding me like this; crushing me up so small?

It would be shown the little yellow veins of gold they were separating, and told it that the precious gold was wanted, and if only a few ounces were got from a ton of quartz it would amply repay them, because they had got all that was good. It is the gold we want to separate and preserve. And that is what God intends by trial to separate the dross from the gold.

It is trial and suffering that God uses to bring out the good there is hid in us. It is painful, but it is necessary. The gold shines but little in the quartz. It is hid, and nothing but crushing will bring it out. There is an aromatic plant waving its leaves and flowers in the air with but little scent. There is the rough pebble picked up on the beach we can see no beauty in it. But put the quartz into mill and furnace, crush the aromatic plant, cut and polish the pebble, and what follows? Bright and shining gold from the quartz, fragrance from the crushed plant, and splendid fair colours from the polished pebble that has been cut.

"This leaf? This stone? It is thy heart.

It must be crushed by pain and smart,

"It must be cleansed by sorrow's art,

Ere it will yield a fragrance sweet,

Ere it will shine a jewel meet,

To lay before thy dear Lord's feet,"

This world to us is what the measured mile is to the steamship. We are on trial. God places us here, some good, some evil, and has plainly set before us the consequences. If we resist the evil and choose the good - everlasting life; if the evil, punishment and suffering. And we shall proceed to illustrate this.

Our first parents were placed in the Garden of Eden, and permitted to eat of every tree in the garden but one. On the day they disobeyed and eat of it, death was to be the penalty. This was a trial, to prove whether they would be obedient. Satan, the great enemy of mankind, suggested to Eve, that if she eat it, she would become wise, God knowing she would live forever. She looked at the fruit -- how much in a look! -- She saw it was "pleasant to the eye," and immediately the "hand," the willing servant of the eye, "took" the fruit, eat, and gave to Adam. He likewise ate; and thus they did not stand the trial, and both were expelled from Eden.

An old man was sitting by the roadside in Hampshire on a heap of flint stones, with a wire mask over his face, a hammer in his hand, breaking flints into pieces to mend the roads. He was poor, and had applied to the parish for help, and they had set him to work to break these stones. It was very hard work and little pay, and as he was toiling and sweating he cried out, "Oh, Eve, oh, Eve, if it had not been for your taking the forbidden fruit, I should never have had to toil and sweat like this."

The road was rather wide, and the grass grew on each side. A gentleman on horseback was gently walking along on the grass, therefore not heard by the man. He heard him blaming mother Eve, and stopping close to him asked him why he was blaming mother Eve. He replied because it was her fault he had to toil." So are you sure you would not have done the same?" "Oh yes, I am sure I would not." "Well," said the gentleman, "if you are so sure, take off your wire mask, and bring your hammer and come with me." He followed the gentleman until they came to a nice house standing in its own grounds. The gentleman went in, and beckoned for him to follow him. He had to wash and put on another suit of clothes, his old ones, with his hammer and mask, being put away carefully together. He was shown a room where he was to stop, and another where he would have his meals, but there would be a dish in the middle of the table that was never to be touched, also a garden in which he might walk. He thanked the gentleman for his kindness, assuring him he would never touch the dish. He soon made himself comfortable, and when the dinner came in there was one dish with the cover in the middle. He said to himself. "This is all I could wish for, I have no need to trouble about that dish;" and so he went on very comfortably for some time. Then he began to think about the cover. "I wonder what can be under it?" Then he thought, "What good would it do me to know? I promised never to touch it." Yet every day the desire to know what was under the cover grew stronger, and one day the desire was so strong that he yielded, and just lifted the cover, when out jumped a mouse. Endeavouring to catch it he fell over a chair. Hearing a noise, the gentleman came in, and seeing in an instant what had happened, said immediately to him. "Change your clothes for your old ones, and take your hammer and wire mask; leave this place, and be sure you never again blame mother Eve when you are breaking stones."

How easy it is for us to be hard upon others and say, "I would not have done it." A poor little hungry boy, without father or mother, and in a starving condition, stole some bread. And one who never knew what want was, said what a bad boy, to take what was not his. Yes, it was wrong; but you do not know how long and how bravely he had struggled against it. Should we have done as much? Peter said to Jesus, "Though they all forsake you I never will." Jesus, Who knew him, said, "Before the cock crow twice thou shalt deny Me thrice." Peter did not stand the trial, but it did him good. He was too confident of his own strength, and was shown how a servant girl could ridicule him into a denial of his Master.

Achan, when he saw the wedge of gold and a goodly Babylonish garment, his covetous desire was awakened, and he took them and hid them under the earth in his tent. His trial was too much. He yielded instead of resisting. He did wrong, hoping to get rich quickly, and brought himself to ruin.

When Ulysses was coming home from the siege of Troy he stopped at an island, where Circe gave him some advice how to escape from the lures of those three Sirens, who were very beautiful, and sat on the rock, and sang so very sweetly that the sailors were enticed to land and were killed. She told Ulysses to fill the ears of his men with white wax, so that they might be deaf to the sweet tones of their voices; but he was not to put it into his own, but he was to get his men to fasten him to the mast with a rope, and if they saw him struggle to get free, they were to get another rope and fasten him more strongly than before, and keep it until they were out of danger. Then they pulled away like Greeks to pass the island. The Sirens sang so sweetly, but they were deaf to their sweet tones, and safely passed the danger.

Beware of the siren voices. How sweetly they sound, all to draw you out of the right way. Our ears must be stopped to their voices, but ever be kept open to hear the sweeter voice that calls so lovingly, "This is the way, walk ye in it. I am the Good Shepherd Who will fold and feed you."

But there is another account of Ulysses and the Sirens; that he had on board his ship Orpheus, who could play the lyre, and had a beautiful loud voice, and he sang so loud and so sweet, that he drowned the Siren voices; so they were not heard, and they got safely by.

We read in the Old Book about Jehoshaphat, the King of Judah, being invaded by an immense army of Edomites, Moabites, and Ammonites. He marched against them, the singers in front, and they struck up and sang, "Praise the Lord, for His mercy endureth for ever," and they were put to confusion; and the Moabite and Ammonite soldiers fell upon the Edomites and utterly destroyed them, and then they fell upon each other. Judah's song was a better one than the Sirens'.

At the Battle of Dunbar, September 2nd, 1650, when General Leslie's army fled before the charge of Oliver Cromwell's soldiers under the first rays of the rising sun, Oliver exclaimed, "Let God arise, let His enemies be scattered!" Cromwell called a halt at the foot of Doon's Hill for the horse to come up. "Now," said he, "let us sing the one hundred and seventeenth psalm"

"O give ye praise unto the Lord

All nations that be,

Likewise, ye people all,

Accord His name to magnify!

"For great to us ward ever are

His loving kindnesses:

His truth endures for evermore,

The Lord 0 do ye bless."

And then the chase to Bellheven, even towards Haddington, and a complete victory was gained. There was a picture in last year's exhibition (1888) at the Royal Academy ("Cromwell at Dunbar") of the halting of Cromwell with eyes lifted heavenward singing this Psalm. There was holy resolution and courage in their faces, taking inspiration from their song.

Glorious are the songs we have heard, and if we sing for Jesus, that will help us in the day of trial. I well remember Philip Phillips, the singing pilgrim, leading an immense audience to sing years since:

"I will sing for Jesus,

With His blood He bought me;

And all along my pilgrim way

His loving hand has brought me.

"Can there overtake me

Any dark disaster,

While I sing for Jesus,

My blessed, blessed Master?

"I will sing for Jesus

His name alone prevailing

Shall be my sweetest music,

When heart and flesh are failing.

"Still I'll sing for Jesus.

Oh, how will I adore Him

Among the cloud of witnesses

Who cast their crowns before Him!

Oh, help me sing for Jesus,

Help me tell the story

Of Him Who did redeem us,

The Lord of life and glory."

The best of all songs are the songs of Zion. Let us praise Him for enabling us to pass through some trials, and ask Him for strength for the future. There are Siren voices that would draw us aside to the music hall, or theatre; don't listen. A minister whom I know, and who is fond of music, was warned by a loving mother never to let his love of music lead him to the theatre or music hall. Once coming by Drury Lane Theatre, he stood to listen to the sound, when, his mother's warning voice sounding in his ears, he heard no more, but walked on.

There are trials of all kinds that come upon us, even upon children. Most are fond of sweets, and if there is an opportunity of quietly helping themselves unseen, how powerful the natural appetite appeals. To another who did not care for sweets it would be no trial at all. The grand question ever should be, "Is it right?" If not right, resist; don't yield to the temptation. Resist the devil, and he will flee from you.

It was the first temptation to Jesus. When He had fasted forty days He was un-hungered. What a sharp thorn is hunger! Do we wonder when children are crying for bread at their parents' grief? What an affecting cry for parents to hear, "Oh, I am so hungry!" It is the natural appetite; and this is the way the great tempter approached Jesus, wanting Him to turn the stones into bread. So we see He was tempted in all points like as we are, yet without sin. To go through a trial and overcome makes us stronger for the next.

"Yield not to temptation, for yielding is sin,

Each victory will help you some other to win;

Fight manfully onward, dark passions subdue,

Look ever to Jesus, He'll carry you through.

Ask the Saviour to help you,

Comfort, strengthen, and keep you,

He is willing to aid you,

He will carry you through."

Jesus was "led of the Spirit into the wilderness." Let us be sure we are led, and not running into temptation. Peter rushed when he went to warm himself. What business had he there? What!

Go into the Hall of Judgment, and sit there among them? Yes, and by their fire. He might have pleaded he wanted to follow his Master, but it was afar off. He was wrong, and suffered miserably. Go nowhere where we cannot pray, "Lord, lead us not into temptation."

Jesus in the wilderness was lonely, yet He was tempted. Some of the early fathers of the Church withdrew from the world, and lived in deserts and caves to lead holy lives, yet they were tempted. How foolish to think of escaping trials! Better to manfully conquer them. Christ's second temptation rose higher,--the first in the wilderness, the second on a pinnacle of the temple, the third higher still, "on a mountain." And the temptations seemed so plausible, "Make these stones bread." Well, then, you are hungry, and need no bread; surely then to descend from the pinnacle you need no stairs. "Throw yourself down." "Thou shalt not tempt the Lord thy God." Satan would have turned his trust into presumption. He could quote Scripture but leave out a part: "To keep thee in all thy ways."

The third temptation rose from pride to ambition. "He showed Him all the kingdoms of the earth in a moment of time."

"All this will I give Thee if Thou wilt fall down and worship me." He showed Him all the glory of them, but not the sorrow and shame of them.

The answer of Jesus was, "Get thee hence, Satan, for it is written, Thou shalt worship the Lord thy God, and only Him shalt thou serve."

The devil left Him, and angels came and ministered unto Him. So if we resist and overcome we shall find joy and peace which will be like angels' visits.

There is a man walking erect carrying a beam of timber. When nearer I found it was a cross. He carried it as if it was no weight, with a firm step and heavenly countenance, and singing a song of the better land. Every time I met him he wore the same happy, cheerful-looking countenance; but I lost sight of him for a long time, and then what a change. He looked so melancholy, with a careworn, wrinkled face, stooping under the weight of the cross. Oh, what a burden, and his song so melancholy! I asked him the reason. He stopped, put down the cross, pulled out a key, and unlocked a cupboard in the cross, and it was so full of gold as not to leave room for another coin." What is this?" said I." Well, I thought it was right to save to provide for my children, but it has made the cross so heavy." "And what else?" He unlocked another, and it was full of tickets for the theatre and sacred concerts. "What is this?" "The cares and anxieties of business were so harassing and worrying that my friends thought I wanted recreation--my mind released from the cares." He then unlocked another, and it contained club tickets for Saturday evenings, "when a few meet together, our minds free from the worries of business." Whether there was anything else that added to the weight of the cross I do not know, but hearing the church bells strike out, he sorrowfully lifted up the cross on his shoulder, and said," I shall be late." He went on singing his melancholy song. I watched him until out of sight. What a picture of many who yielded to trials one after another, until, though sound in creed, all the life and vitality was eaten out of their religion, that it was only a name to live.

Oh, resist these Siren voices, and you shall, through God's grace, overcome. He is ever on the watch. Beware of the beginnings, the thin edge of the wedge. He will help you to conquer all. Only trust Him and seek His help.

The grand lesson to be learnt here is the weapon that Jesus used in the conflict. It was "the Word of God," the sword of the Spirit. Let our minds be stored with it, hid in our hearts, read every day, pondered and thought over. What a glorious revelation that "God so loved the world as to give His only begotten Son, that whosoever believeth on Him should not perish, but have everlasting life." It reveals more still, -- that He became" one of us," took upon Him our nature, was" touched with a feeling of our infirmities, and tempted in all points like as we are, yet without sin," therefore He is able to succour those that are tempted. He is full of sympathy and love, knows all about us. Look ever to Him.

"Shun evil companions, bad language disdain,

God's name bold in reverence, nor take it in vain,

Be thoughtful and earnest, kind-hearted and true;

Look ever to Jesus, He'll carry you through.

To him who overcometh God giveth a crown,

Through faith we shall conquer though often cast down;

He who is our Saviour our strength will renew;

Look ever to Jesus, He'll carry you through."

Trial is necessary for us all. Sometimes a piece of ironwork has an important part to perform, and it is necessary it should be sound, no flaws, as a piston-rod of an engine or axle-tree of a carriage; and if there is suspicion of one, then plunge it into the fire and make it red hot, then the flaw will be seen. The fire will show it. So nothing but fire will prove us and show our defects. To remove the dross. "For He shall sit as a refiner and purifier of silver: and He shall purify the sons of Levi, that they may offer unto the Lord an offering in righteousness." Trial is to strengthen and enable us to overcome. For the grandest sight in the universe is to see a youth struggling to do right amidst opposition and ridicule. Then struggle on, and you shall be "snore than conquerors through Him that loved you."

The Rev. John Newton had been a dreadful bad character, a sailor sunk in vice, but when converted he was turned right round, and became a holy good minister of Jesus Christ. He wrote this beautiful hymn about trials: --

"I asked the Lord that I might grow

In faith and love and every grace;

Might more of His salvation know,

And seek more earnestly His face.

"Twas He Who taught me thus to pray,

And He, I trust, has answer'd prayer;

But it has been in such a way.

As almost drove me to despair.

"I hoped that in some favoured hour

At once He'd answer my request;

And by His love's restraining power.

Subdue my sins and give me rest.

"Instead of this -- He made me feel.

The hidden evils of my heart,

And let the angry powers of hell

Assault my soul in every part.

"Yea, more, with His own hand He seem'd

Intent to aggravate my woe,

Cross'd all the fair designs I schem'd,

Blasted my gourds, and laid me low.

"'Lord, why is this?' I trembling cried;

'Wilt Thou pursue Thy worm to death?

'Tis in this way,' the Lord replied,

'I answer prayer for grace and faith.

"'These inward trials I employ,

From pride and self to set thee free;

And break thy schemes of earthly joy,

That thou may'st seek thy all in Me.''

This is God's mysterious way of dealing with us. "No trial for the present is joyous but grievous, but after it will work out the peaceable fruits of righteousness." Let us also remember that He will not let any temptation befall us without making a way of escape; and if we suffer painfully, the rod is in the hands of our heavenly Father, Who will not lay it on us above what we are able to bear." He sits as the refiner of silver." Sitting denotes earnest attention to what is before him. The refiner, in an ancient sculpture, is shown sitting before a furnace watching the pot with the silver. What for? To get rid of the dross; and when the refiner can see his face in the surface he knows the silver is pure. So when the dross is removed, He will see us reflect His face and image; then the furnace is no longer needed; trial has had its purpose -- to purify, and then we shall realise the blessing. For" Blessed are the pure in heart, for they shall see God."

"God moves in a mysterious way

His wonders to perform,

He plants His footsteps on the sea,

And rides upon the storm."

CHAPTER V

"AND IT WAS WINTER."

A SWISS gentleman, who was accustomed to the grand mountain scenery of his own country, and had travelled much, said to a friend of mine, that when he arrived at the top of Olivet, and Jerusalem suddenly burst upon his view, that it was the grandest of all the scenes he had ever gazed upon.

Richard I., Coeur de Lion, who went with a crusading army to recover Jerusalem from the hands of the Saracens, when he caught sight of the Holy City from the same spot, is said to have placed his hands before his eyes and exclaimed, "Let me never see thee, except I win thee."

A greater than Richard once sat upon this mountain gazing upon the city when it was far more glorious in appearance. It was Jesus, surrounded by His disciples, and the temple before them, as beautified by Herod during forty-six years, rose in all its majesty and grandeur. Conspicuous were those large stones of white marble, decorated with plates of silver, glittering in the rays of the sun, so dazzling to the eyes of the spectators as to make unknown warrior...

Left Him, and angels came and ministered unto Him. So if we resist and overcome we shall find joy and peace which will be like angels' visits.

There is a man walking erect carrying a bearer of timber. When nearer I found it was a cross. He carried it as if it was no weight, with a firm step and heavenly countenance, and singing a song of the better latency. Every time I met him he afore the same happy, cheerful-looking countenance; but I lost sight of him for a long time, and then what a change. He looked so melancholy, with a careworn, wrinkled face, stooping under the weight of the cross. Oh, what a burden, and his song so melancholy! I asked him the reason. He stopped, put down the cross, pulled out, a key, and unlocked. a cupboard in the cross, and it was so full of gold as not to leave room for another coin. "What is this?" said I. "Well, I thought it vas right to save to provide for my children, but it has made the cross so heavy."

"And what else?" He unlocked another, and it was full of tickets for the theatre and sacred concerts. "What is this?" "The cares and anxieties of business were so harassing and worrying that my friends thought I wanted recreation--my mind released from the cares." He then unlocked another; and it contained club tickets for Saturday evenings, "when a few meet together, our minds free from the worries of business." Whether there was anything else that added to the weight of the cross I do not know, but hearing the church bells strike out, he sorrowfully lifted up the cross on his shoulder, and said," 1 shall be late." He went on singing his melancholy song. I watched him until out of sight. What a picture of many who yielded to trials one after another, until, though sound in creed, all the life and vitality was eaten out, of their religion, that it was only a name to live.

Oh, resist these Siren voices, and you shall, through God's grace, overcome. He is ever on the watch. Beware of the beginnings, the thin edge of the wedge. He will help you to conquer all. Only trust Him and seek His help.

The grand lesson to be learnt here is the weapon that Jesus used in the conflict. It was "the Word of God," the sword of the Spirit. Let our minds be stored with it, hid in our hearts, read every day, pondered and thought over. What a glorious revelation that God so loved the world as to give His only begotten Son, that whosoever believeth on Him should not, perish, but have everlasting life." It reveals more still, that He became "one of us," took upon Him our nature, was" touched with a feeling of our infirmities, and tempted in all points like as eve are, yet without sin," therefore He is able to succour those that are tempted. He is full of sympathy and love, knows all about us.

Look ever to Him then turn aside their gaze. Here stood Solomon's Porch, built on the top of the high wall facing the valley and mountain. Well might the disciples call their Master's attention to "these great stones" and "what manner of buildings." Josephus, who saw them, says they were forty-three feet long, twenty-one feet wide, and fourteen feet thick. They might well say "these stones;" and He sorrowfully told them that in a few years there would not remain one stone upon another.

Solomon's Porch was one of the outer courts of the temple, but covered in, and Jesus often walked here with His disciples, and taught the people, and one reason is here given why -- "and it was winter."

How wonderful is the course of seasons! Our annual course round the sun at a speed of nearly twenty miles in a second of time gives us spring, summer, autumn, and winter, and our daily revolution of six hundred miles an hour gives us day and night. Did you ever notice the turning of a grindstone? If it is turned fast it throws the water off; if it is turned at moderate speed it just keeps the water on; if slowly the water remains at the bottom. What wisdom there is in the exact speed of the earth and all these arrangements! Our daily revolution gives us night and day, night for rest and day for labour; and in the vegetable kingdom summer for growth, and winter for rest.

Spring flowers, summer fruits, and autumn corn are all gathered, and cold winter has come like a deep sleep over the face of the country. The trees are bare, and the wintry winds moan and whistle through the bare branches. Some animals have to live on the stores they have saved up during the summer and autumn, -- the squirrel upon his store of sound nuts gathered carefully, the dormouse upon his stock of grains of corn, and bees and wasps upon their honey. Others are hybernating; that is, they are in a state of torpor or sleep, and require nothing to eat, as the bats who hang themselves up by the little hooks on their wings in the hollow of some old tree or old ruin. The Bible speaks of winter. Jacob complained of "being consumed by frost at night," and the Psalmist exclaims, "He giveth snow like wool," " He scattereth the hoar frost like ashes" " He casteth forth his ice like morsels," "Who can stand before His cold?" " He saith to the snow, be thou upon the earth." We are told of a man killing a lion in the time of snow, and of "the snows of Lebanon," the melting of which cause the overflow of the river Jordan. The Rev. A. Hall told me he rode into Jerusalem in a blinding snowstorm; and Peter coming to warm himself by the fire at night incidentally tells us of the cold in the hills of Judea; and when we think that Jesus spent whole nights on the mountain side,

"Cold mountains and the midnight air

Witnessed the fervour of His prayer,"

How wonderful are the effects of cold! When the thermometer falls below thirty-two the liquid water becomes congealed, like glass -- it is frozen; and if there is any moisture in the air, the cold freezes it, and it becomes snow formed into flakes.

Some Frenchmen were wintering at Tornau in and, and when the door of their hut was opened, moisture of their breath formed instantly into flakes of snow.

How wonderful are flakes of snow, how beautiful their forms! Scoresby, Glaisher, and others observed nearly a thousand different shapes, mostly six-pointed stars. And a large flake is sometimes or mostly formed of several smaller ones clinging to each other, and all of different shapes.

And how white! How is this? It is the result of the combination of the different prismatic rays issuing from these minute snow crystals. We see the same on the white foam of the sea on the top he waves.

The sea may look blue or green, but no sooner is it agitated by the wind than waves are formed, and small spray or foam is broken into such small titles, that the light is reflected by them; and in, break a black glass bottle, grind it to powder, it becomes white, the minute particles reflect-the light. The purest white we can make, how pure compared to snow! How dirty the whitest as when the house tops are covered with snow!

You may ask, "What is the use of snow?" Falling immense quantities, and thence, by its gradual melting, it steadily and quietly feeds the springs, and through them the streams and rivers, which a heavy fall of rain would convert into fearfully destructive torrents, sweeping over whole tracts of entry. In some countries the snow tempers the burning heats by cooling the breezes that come over the snow and that pass to the warm plains below, and in temperate zones all vegetation of winter is protected by a fall of snow. It has been found in this country that Alpine plants brought from Switzerland frequently perish from the cold here, though not so cold as their native place, because they do not get the annual covering of snow that keeps them warm and screens them from the frost; and spread over the grain fields it protects the tender shoots and the roots from the action of severe frosts. It is not only

"Beautiful snow, beautiful snow,"

But useful too. God sends it, as well as rain and sunshine, on a kindly errand.

Snow is an emblem of purity. "Though your sins were as scarlet, they shall be whiter than snow." The colour can never be got out of scarlet material; scarlet rags will only make the pinkish blotting paper, or with a tinge of red. What a change from scarlet to white; yes, and whiter than snow.

What a lesson from a snowflake! It is the power of little things; despise nothing because it is small. Snowflakes are very small, but it is the multitude of them, and their continuous fall, that gives them the power. Even whilst writing this there has been a fall of snow for a few hours, blocking up the thoroughfares, stopping the traffic of the streets, throwing into disorder between four and five millions of people in this great city of London. What God can do when "He casteth forth His snow like wool." Who can stop Him? How puny are our efforts! -

An avalanche is an immense body of snow overhanging the great precipice, sometimes more than one hundred feet thick; overbalancing, falls or slides down, carrying all before it. In one of the Catholic cantons of Switzerland they cut away the trees above their village, and an avalanche came down and destroyed the whole village, therefore they are forbidden to cut down any trees above the villages or towns, that they may form a snow break. The slightest noise, such as a shout, or letting fall an ice axe, will set the snow in motion. Noise causes a vibration of the air. In certain conditions of the snow the Alpine guides put their fingers to their lips, as much as to say, "Don't speak.

There is also the rolling avalanche. Snow detached and set in motion, as it rolls along, gathers the snow as it rolls over it, and increases its bulk and speed, and carries everything before it.

It is snowflakes that keep the highest mountains in Switzerland covered with snow, and which form the great glaciers containing millions of tons, and which are travelling at the rate of about a foot per day, for a ladder that was left in the snow came out at the bottom of the glacier more than forty years after, also the body of a guide who fell down a crevasse and lost his life, came out at the bottom of the glacier with the colour in his face, as the immense weight of the snow is always pressing it down, and from observation is continually travelling downward. And often the glacier, being very wide, and the space between the high rocks through which the glacier passes very narrow, it presses very hard against the sides, and frequently brings immense blocks of the rock away to the bottoms of the glaciers, where they are left, and called moraines. Fresh snow continually falling fills up the crevasses and covers the tops of the mountains, repairing all the waste. Glaciers have been called "God's ice plough," altering the appearance of the face of the country. Great masses of rock are carried down, and as the glacier melts so it leaves the moraine at the bottom.

Sir Edward Belcher came close to an immense iceberg near the coast of Newfoundland, and great streams of muddy water were running down the sides into the sea. It had probably broken away from some part of the coast of Norway, and brought away a large quantity of earth, gravel, and sand, which as the iceberg melted was deposited at the bottom of the sea. In some parts of England and Scotland masses of rock are found many miles away from any rock of the same kind, and we can only suppose that in ancient times the glaciers did it.

Let us never despise small things. A little kind action, a kind look or word instead of a frown, a smile with an outstretched arm to shake by the hand, what would this produce in one year, if all was in place of the contrary? We should hardly know it, so great would be the change, that it would be like throwing a stone into a pond, which sunk to the bottom, but left a round ring in the water where it sunk, that would be succeeded by ring after ring until they reached the outer edge of the pond.

"Who can stand before His cold?" How sadly this was illustrated in Napoleon's invasion of Russia. His army of upwards of half a million of soldiers advanced irresistibly, notwithstanding the determined opposition of the Russian soldiers, who seemed powerless before him. He took Moscow, the ancient capital of Russia, and installed himself in the Kremlin, the ancient palace of the Russian Czars. But God sent two of His generals against him, General Frost and General Snow, with their immense army, against the Corsican. General Frost advanced from the north, and stopped all the rivers from running, so that no provisions could be moved, and General Snow followed, covering the whole country with a white mantle of snowflakes. He was stopped, and this gave time for the Russian army to gather round him and harass him in every direction. They also set fire to Moscow, making it hardly habitable; and because he could not get his supplies to the front he was at length obliged to retreat. In crossing the Barizina river the bridge was blocked up with baggage, and the Russian Cossacks fired and charged the French, who, not able to get over the bridge, were driven into the freezing river, and the next year when the river thawed thirty-six thousand bodies were taken out. Hundreds and thousands, fatigued and wearied, sat down to rest by the roadside, and dropped into a slumber from which they never woke, being frozen to death. "Who can stand before His cold? "

The untimely fate of Sir John Franklin and his one hundred and thirty-seven brave companions from cold and hunger, is touching in the extreme.

What must have been their sufferings in those cold icy regions! The bodies of some were found in boats; they could drag no further from weakness and cold. The memorials and relics found, and now kept at: Greenwich and elsewhere, tell a most affecting story. I knew the mother of one of these men on the expedition who lost his life. He had, in common with all, double pay, and half pay he left to his mother, who drew it for six years, and then it was stopped, as, receiving no news, the Admiralty believed they were dead.

Also remember what is endured in the winter by our brave seamen in the blinding snowstorms at sea, or by the North Sea fishermen and trawlers who supply your table with fish. And as you have your breakfast by the cheerful fire in the warm room, that most of the things on the table have reached our island home by the brave sailors, who brought them through all kinds of weather, hot and cold, for our comfort. Our tea from China, Assam, etc., sugar, and coffee, and cocoa from East and West Indies, and our bread from nearly every part of the world. Let us never forget them, and cheerfully do all we can to contribute to their welfare. I was glad to see a hospital ship sent to the North Sea for the smack-men and trawlers a short time since. We have Sailors' Homes, Lifeboats, Shipwrecked Sailors' Society, etc.

My brother once doubled Cape Horn, and their bows were covered with snow and ice for many days. Continually are they exposed to the dangers of storms, collisions, and shipwrecks.

"Then, O protect the hardy tar,

Be mindful of his merit."

And yet what wisdom is shown by God in these cold regions. The great whale can thrive and sport amidst the terrible icebergs, for he has a great coat of fat two feet thick to keep him warm. Narwhals, silver foxes, walruses, Polar bears, and musk ox supply food and warm skins for clothing, and the reindeer can draw the Laplander in his sledge, and supply him with buttermilk and venison.

And what wonderful provision God has made for us that we may enjoy the cold and dreary season of the year. The enormous beds of coal that lie buried beneath the surface of our earth were once immense forests of tree-ferns, which overspread our country in bygone ages when the climate was tropical, and the ponds and lakes were inhabited by enormous lizards with eyes as large as a frying-pan, and mouths big enough to take in a dozen persons, seats and all, which, dying, sunk down to the bottom, and their bones became embedded in it, and in the course of ages the mud has hardened into limestone; and in the quarries of Lyme Regis in Dorsetshire the skeletons of these monster lizards are found, the immense remains of which may be seen in the British Museum.

By some convulsions of Nature our earth has passed through it has gradually become fit for the life of man, the last and noblest of God's creation.

No one would like to inhabit a house half finished or unfurnished, and so our heavenly Father did not place us here until He had filled our great coal cellar; and not only coal, but stone, iron, tin, silver, lead, copper, slates, etc., --everything for man's use, and only requiring his labour to get them. Gaze into your coal-scuttle, and behold the black diamonds -- black indeed; but what a beautiful bright light comes from this dark mass.

George Stephenson once asked a lady who was gazing upon a passing train, "Madam, what is driving that train along?" "One of your canny Newcastle drivers, I suppose," was the reply. "No, madam," was his reply;" no, madam, it is bottled up sunbeams." How true it is God never made anything in vain--not even the sunbeams that shone ages ago before the existence of man on those tropical tree-fern forests of Great Britain.

Nothing can be lost. A piece of coal is a wonder, not only containing light and heat, but all the colours of the rainbow, and the most lovely tints are brought out of the refuse of the coal; every beautiful dye is now extracted from it, entirely superseding the vegetable dyes of olden times. Every tint, from the rising to the setting sun in the bygone ages in which the insects of that period lived, gambolled, and died, is now reproduced for our benefit. Not one sunbeam shone in vain. When we think of a piece of coal, a black diamond, we ought to sing,

"Praise God, from whom all blessings flow."

Winter is the time for social gatherings. How cheerful to meet and enjoy the "Feast of reason and the flow of soul." Winter is the time for scarcity of work, poverty, and suffering, when the poor need clothing and food. Let us think of our mercies, and have hearts to feel for others.

What a lesson we learn from the dogs of St. Bernard, the highest inhabited house in Europe. The monks many years since gave their hospitality to a poor Dane, who, to show his gratitude for their great kindness, gave them his fine dog, which was the father of this peculiar race of dogs, now so well known and celebrated throughout the world.

Immediately after a snowstorm the dogs are sent out, mostly in two's. One has a small cask fastened round his neck, and the other carries some warm clothing strapped on. And if a poor traveller was overtaken by the storm and nearly buried in the snow, they set to work to scrape it away, and lay upon him, that the warmth of their bodies might restore him to consciousness and enable him to follow them to the Hospice.

One dog named Barry saved upwards of forty persons. This interesting animal found a boy in a frozen state between the bridge Druoz and the ice house of Balsoa. He immediately began to lick him, and having restored animation and perfect recovery by means of his caresses, he induced him to get on his back, and tie himself on; and in this manner he carried him, as it were, in triumph to the Hospice; and at last Barry died in harness, taking a poor Italian woman and her son through a mountain pass, when an avalanche fell and buried them. Let none of us shrink from going on an errand of mercy for the benefit of others.

Is it cold without? How sad if cold and icy within! Cold and icy hearts, no love -- oh, how chilling! Why, it is the emblem of death. The trees and plants look as if they were dead; and what a true picture of many, "dead in trespasses and sins." Soon will the sun gain strength, shining stronger and stronger, and will soon drive away the cold. So may the Great Sun of Righteousness rise with power. Oh, let the warmth of His love melt all your coldness and fill your hearts with warmth.

The sun in the Arctic regions is seen for three months and then absent for three months. All is ice and snow; hence it is called the "Land of the midnight sun." From this desolate scene let us lift up our thoughts to the region where" the sun never sets." "No night there;" a river of pleasure ever flowing, never frozen; an ocean of felicity that can never be exhausted a day without a night; a spring without a winter; pure, unmingled, spiritual, never-ending felicity.

CHAPTER VI

THE LOST SAYING FOUND.

SOME travellers were walking along the banks of the river that rushes over the Falls of Niagara, when they saw a canoe in mid-stream, apparently with no one in it, rapidly nearing the falls. "I wonder if any one is in the canoe?" was the inquiry of one; and immediately they all climbed the highest bank to see, and the conclusion they came to was that there was something in the bottom, whether a man, woman, or a bundle of things, they could not tell; it might be a living person. What was to be done? There was no time to lose. One of the party, a strong swimmer, offered to swim out to the boat with a rope round his body, so as to get into the canoe and fasten the rope to the thwarts, and they, by their united strength, pull them to the shore; but if he failed to reach her, they were to pull him to the bank. Being a strong swimmer, he soon reached the canoe, and found a woman in a swoon lying in the bottom. Making the rope fast he gave the signal, and the canoe was pulled to the bank with her living freight, and by the timely use of restoratives soon brought her round, and she recovered. She was just snatched from going over the fall into the seething cauldron below.

That is just like "the lost saying found," the motto for this chapter. All that we know about the Lord Jesus Christ is to be found in the Four Gospels, and a few incidents handed down to us through the Epistles; and John tells us, in the concluding verses of his Gospel," That if all the Lord Jesus had said and done were recorded, the world itself would not contain the books that recorded them." What a busy life His was! But there is one saying of the Lord Jesus Christ's, just like the woman in the canoe, who was being swiftly swept to oblivion, but brought out some one's memory and told the Apostle Paul, who, when he was taking leave of the elders of Ephesus on the seashore, said this, "Remembering the words of the Lord Jesus Christ, How it is more blessed to give than to receive." How strange this will sound to the young, especially at Christmas, New Year, or on birthdays, the special seasons for expecting and receiving gifts. How they seem to be dissolved into thin air by these startling words of the Lord Jesus. And all those who, like Mr. Micawber, are waiting "for something to turn up," these words seem to cut away at one blow all their fancied happiness. It seems to have turned the world upside down. There is another startling truth hanging on to this, "That it is impossible to give without receiving."

What will most children do? Imitate others, especially those that are older. They will put on grandfather's nightcap or grandmother's spectacles, or do something that father or mother does; they also imitate that which is bad, learn bad language. We should all strive to imitate the noble, wise, and good; but above all, in our humble way, imitate God.

Suppose we went into a sculptor's gallery, and there was a beautiful statue of white marble, which only seemed as if waiting to receive life.

On the floor is a heap of clay for us to use to model another like it. After long labour we succeed, and make one something like it, but it is only clay, and a poor imitation. So our imitation of God's giving is only as clay compared to marble, but we must try to improve with every trial.

How does God give? In many ways, and to none exactly alike. To some He gives enlarged information; to others great powers of memory, or strength and power to work, to keep plodding on, or, as General Grant termed, "to keep pegging away;" to some money; to others the power of getting it. Some He puts into a good social position, and others He surrounds with kind parents and an affectionate circle of friends. Then He gives health— the best of blessings—and some rejoice in their strength. Then have pity on the weak.

Have you bright and sunny homes? God gave them to you. Think of those dark and cloudy. Are you sharp at learning? Never call another a dunce who cannot learn so fast as you do. God gave you the power of intellect. What a wreck is a man or woman without an intellect! Think of the madhouses with their many intellects thus deranged, and praise God for intellect.

And God has given us all something we never did anything to get. Our forefathers fought, suffered, bled, and died, to procure the liberties we now enjoy. They were imprisoned and died in dungeons, turned out of their homes, becoming fugitives and wanderers, and many died under the privations and sufferings they endured; others were burned at the stake, — all to procure us our Bible and our religion, as well as our civil liberties. Let us receive them as a precious inheritance. Take care of our Bibles — read them, love them; for it is a revelation of God's greatest gift by the greatest of all givers.

What does God give to all? Rain and sunshine, light and warmth, day and night, summer and winter. His mercies are like the dew — copious, yet so gently bestowed as scarcely to be felt. Do you go to bed with an aching head? Yes; but you rise quite refreshed. "He giveth His beloved sleep." How often ought we to sing" Praise God, from whom all blessings flow"! He has given the sun, moon, and stars, the mighty ocean, the flowing river, the lofty mountain, the fertile valley, delicious fruit and glorious flowers, charming the eye, and delicious in perfume. He has given enjoyments to all creation, from the elephant and hippopotamus, down to the ephemera or Mayfly, whose brief existence is one hour on an evening in May.

How does He give? Freely. We often give to get something in return. That's not giving freely. There is an old saying, "There is no grace in the gift that sticks to the finger." And many give for a name, for if it is published in the paper they give.

If not, their pocket is tightly buttoned up. Some give to get.

A smuggler met a customs officer, and wanting to get some spirit casks and bales of silk away, said, "I suppose if I was to put a guinea over each of your eyes you would not see." "No," he said. "And if you put one over each ear, I should hear nothing." This is a bad gift to both giver and receiver. Persons who hold situations of trust are bribed to do for others what is not right; and to such a shameful state was the corruption in the English Parliament, that Horace Walpole boasted that he knew the price of every member.

What is the greatest of all God's gifts? "God so loved the world, that He gave His only begotten Son, that whosoever believeth on Him should not perish but have everlasting life." What a gift!

God punishes greedy, selfish people that will not give, and they lose all the blessedness that belongs to giving. Many years ago the Dutch cut down all the spice trees in an island to make the spice scarce and keep up the price. But what followed? The island became so unhealthy that they could not live on it until the trees had grown again. And Cowper tells of the greedy landlord, who was not satisfied with the hamper of pippins his cottager gave him, but wanted the pippin-tree, and at the proper time took it up and removed it to his own garden. But the tree would not take root in the new soil, so he lost his pippins and the tree as well.

"'Oh,' he cried, 'I had been content

With tribute small indeed, but kindly meant!

My avarice has expensive proved to me,

Has cost me both my pippins and the tree.'"

Now we will give some illustrations of the blessedness of giving. A poor boy, without father and mother, and living with his poor grandmother, went to market every morning to buy violets to make into button-holes, to sell to gentlemen going to their city offices, and earned just enough to keep him from being a burden to his aged grandmother. As he generally invested all his money in violets, he was unable to have his breakfast until he had sold enough to get it. One morning it was very cold, and he did not sell a single bunch. Probably going supperless to bed he was cold and hungry, and burst into tears. When a kind-hearted lady asked him why he was crying, he told her. She gave him twopence to run and get a loaf whilst she held his violets. He soon returned, and taking his violets went down a side street, sitting down on a doorstep to eat it. She thought she would watch him from where he could not see her. She saw him eat the loaf with that true enjoyment that only a hungry lad can show. Presently a hungry-looking dog came and sat down in front of him, wagged his tail, and looked up wistfully in the boy's face. The boy pitied the dog, and breaking off a piece of bread gave it to him." That was a kind action for a hungry boy," thought the lady. "I will inquire more about him, and see if his story is true." She found it was, became his friend, gave him a start, and being a steady, industrious boy, he rose up, and became a steady rising man.

He did not see any connection between giving a hungry dog a piece of bread and his rising in society, by making that lady his friend to help him on in the world. But there was. We do not see all the links in the chain of events, but they are there, connecting the giving with the receiving.

A poor Macedonian was daily employed with his donkey, taking stores to the palace. One day it was an extra heavy load, there being a considerable quantity of gold for the palace expenses. The poor donkey seemed ready to drop, when his kind and considerate master took it from his back, put it upon his own, and was staggering along with it, when Alexander, who had been watching him, walked up, and quietly touching him on the shoulder said," Friend, carry it a little farther, to thine own tent, for it is all thine own."

He did not see the connection between helping a poor donkey and getting a fortune, but there was.

The working men of Edinburgh and Glasgow, wishing to perpetuate the name of Ballantyne, clubbed together and built a lifeboat with the name of Edinburgh and Ballantyne, in honour of the author of "The Lifeboat," and on December 17th, 1866, it was to be seen near the Broomielaw, Glasgow, on show; and suspended also on the wall was a box to receive the contributions of those visitors who should call to see the lifeboat, and wish to lend a hand toward her outfit, which wanted completing, and to help keeping her when afloat. Among those who came to see her before she was sent to her station, Port Logan, on the Wigtownshire coast, was the wife of the captain of the bark Strathlevin, accompanied by her children.

A sailor's wife and children would naturally look at the lifeboat with different feelings from a landsman. I was born on the sea, and remember how on stormy nights were heard, tales of perils in the deep. One can imagine the stories of the dangers of the sea those boys had listened to, and whilst looking at the boat, the thought may, and probably did, come," If father was in such a plight, and his life hanging on the strength of the arm that was taking such gallant strokes with the sea." So she lifted up her boys one after the other to drop the silver coins she had just taken out of her pocket into the box for the fund.

This is a very simple story — yes; but exactly one year after this, December 17th, 1867, a bark was caught in the cold, wild weather off the Wigtownshire coasts, and driven on the rocks. The situation was desperate. The vessel would soon break up; the fifteen souls who clung to her rigging saw, that unless they were soon rescued death must be their fate; but happily they were seen by watchers on shore, and very soon the captain of the Strathlevin saw the lifeboat coming, for the vessel was none other than the Glasgow bark Strathlevin, and the captain was the husband of the lady who lifted up her sons to drop the money into the box that was to set the craft in motion. But this was not all the marvels of that strange coincidence. When the lifeboat warped alongside, and took the fifteen helpless sailors off the wreck safely, she proved to be none other than the Port Logan lifeboat, with the well-known name of Ballantyne painted in the stern sheets; and so the captain of the Strathlevin came safe to his home instead of his corpse drifting out in the rolling North Sea, with all his ship's company. He had to tell his glad and happy wife, and that "tiny public," his children, who had heard "mother's little lecture on lifeboats," that on the same day of the month, but a year later on, that they gave their money for love and charity to the boat, that selfsame boat had saved him from death, and sent him alive and grateful to their arms.

Some may call this "chance" or coincidence. Do we not catch the Divine administration of good for good and evil for evil? Cannot we imagine the angel with the golden scales weighing all our deeds and thoughts, and paying for them? What did the Scotch captain's wife's silver pay for? What connected the first shining link of pity and womanly feeling with the last link of manly gallantry and timely service at the other end of the chain of events? If we knew, as the angels know, that the very coin dropped in paid for a halliard, or a tow-line that had to do with the rescue, or a spare rowlock that saved a minute in starting, or some other cause that led to the beautiful issue, we should see that the human love and pity which prompted the gift of the mother are indeed potent forces, infinite in power and result. No good action ever dies. Although we do not see the middle links of the great chain, we do the two ends, and our faith in the good shows us the connecting centre part.

"We see through a glass darkly," but God the end from the beginning.

There is a Jewish tradition that when Moses was in the Mount God permitted him to ask some questions about His government of the world. Moses was told to look down into a valley, and he saw a fountain of water. A soldier came riding up, and after he and his horse had drank, he sat down to rest, and pulling out his purse, looked into it, and put it down by his side. After a short rest he arose, attended to his horse, mounted, and rode off, forgetting all about his purse. Shortly after a little child came, and seeing the purse, took it away. A few minutes after, an old man, tired and weary, with difficulty tottered up to the fountain and sat down to rest. The soldier, having missed his purse, rode back, and finding the old man sitting at the fountain, accused him of taking the purse. He protested his innocence, but the soldier did not believe him, and drew his sword and killed him on the spot.

Moses shuddered at the sight, and wondered the Almighty should permit such injustice. The reply was, "Stop, Moses. Did you see that child take the purse? Know that the old man was the murderer of that child's father."

There is a chain of events that brings the wrongdoer to punishment in some singular way. Strange was the way Jacob received punishment for deceiving his father. All through his life he was the victim of deception. His father-in-law, Laban, cheated him out of seven years' service for his daughter Rachel. He changed his wages ten times, and last, and worst of all, he was deceived by his own children. There is indeed a connecting link between wrongdoing and the punishment that surely follows it.

The ancients believed in a goddess they called Nemesis or Retribution, that followed our evil doings, dogged our footsteps, and punished our misdeeds in such a way as to bring them home to us. And so there are blessings following giving in the way of receiving.

Alfred the Great was once so short of provisions that he had only one loaf left, and a hungry beggar came and asked for relief. He gave him their all, and very shortly after his men returned from a forage bringing abundance. He gave and soon received.

A little English girl was sent to Paris to school that she might speak the language purely. One evening she accompanied her schoolfellows for a walk through the Passy gate where a soldier was on guard, who asked them to get him something to drink. They refused proudly, thinking it beneath them to wait upon a soldier, but the little English maid ran and got him some water. He drank it, and feeling better he thanked his little benefactress, and asked her what was her name? He put it down; and, where did she live? That he also noted down. That night was the St. Bartholomew Massacre. That soldier went to her house and saved her. She only gave a cup of cold water, but received her life and safety.

God sees the whole of our actions, and regards the very least of them. At the last great day Jesus is described as saying to those on His right hand, "Come, ye blessed of My Father, inherit the kingdom prepared for you before the foundation of the world. For I was hungered, and ye gave Me meat, I was thirsty, and ye gave Me drink. I was a stranger, and ye took Me in. Naked, and ye clothed Me. I was sick and in prison, and ye visited Me." But they answered Him, saying, "Lord, when saw we Thee hungry or thirsty, or a stranger, or naked, or sick, or in prison?" Then the King shall answer," Inasmuch as ye did it unto one of the least of these, My brethren, ye did it unto Me." The smallest kind action never passes unobserved.

It is the custom in some of our Sunday Schools to subscribe ten pounds a year to the Missionary Society to keep a native teacher, who is named after some departed friend or some living teacher or friend whose name it was desirous to keep in fragrant memory. Many of these teachers are in the South Sea Islands, and are sent as pioneers to prepare the way for the English missionary; and how often God has blessed their labours and quite changed the whole population. I have a coloured picture of the natives of Savage Island given me by my brother who visited the island somewhere between 1844 and 1849. It is by the draughtsman of their surveying staff, and they were in a truly savage state. Now they are clothed and in their right minds. They have chapels and schools, and all the young can read their Bibles; and all this is to be ascribed to the work of the native teachers.

How many brothers of those who subscribed to a native teacher have been saved when shipwrecked on these islands by the changes brought about by the native teachers, with God's blessing; so the money paid to support the native teachers came back with interest when they heard that some of the crew came from the very school that kept the native teacher, who was the means of bringing about all the kindness the shipwrecked crew received. What a mysterious connection between giving and receiving.

Christ loved His Church, and gave Himself for it, and the influence should be the consecration of it; and individually we should give ourselves, and give "now," "now;" not at any future time, but "now." Ah! That will be a blessed gift; and what in return? God gives everlasting life. Think just for one moment of what is given in return, and you must exclaim, "Verily it is more blessed to give than to receive." For we receive infinitely more than we give.

Some one asked Alexander to give him a large sum of money, and he instantly gave it. Some of his courtiers remonstrated with him on the folly of giving his money to any one who asked him, and giving all they asked for. He replied," If it was not too much for them to ask, it was not too much for an Alexander to give.

God gives royally, like a king." If any man lack wisdom," (and who does not?) "let him ask of God, who giveth liberally and upbraideth not."

He gives like a king, but more royally, more princely, more liberally. He gives everlasting life, obtained only through the gift of His own dear Son. The Apostle Paul was lost in rapture when he heard of it and thought of it. He burst out, "Thanks be to God for His unspeakable gift."

God now says again, "See how wonderfully I have formed you, put you in a world of wonders, given you a wonderful box that cannot be destroyed, marvellous lids to let in and out, wonderful servants to help, and a heart that should have a cluster of the sweetest affections." Give, and give to the Royal Giver. A French soldier was wounded by a. musket ball, and the surgeons were probing the wound deeply to find the ball, when he cried out, "Probe a little deeper, and you will find the Emperor," as much as to say that the Emperor possessed the very inmost and deepest of his heart's affections, that he was entirely the Emperor's. This is the giving, the thorough devotion that God requires. Give, and enjoy the blessedness.

CPSIA information can be obtained at www.ICGtesting.com
Printed in the USA
LVOW09s1556120215

426800LV00030B/1363/P

9 781496 107732